HAGGAI, ZECHARIAH, AND MALACHI

CASCADE COMPANIONS

The Christian theological tradition provides an embarrassment of riches: from Scripture to modern scholarship, we are blessed with a vast and complex theological inheritance. And yet this feast of traditional riches is too frequently inaccessible to the general reader.

The Cascade Companions series addresses the challenge by publishing books that combine academic rigor with broad appeal and readability. They aim to introduce nonspecialist readers to that vital storehouse of authors, documents, themes, histories, arguments, and movements that comprise this heritage with brief yet compelling volumes.

RECENT TITLES IN THIS SERIES:

Cascade Companion to Evil by Charles Taliaferro
Metaphysics by Donald Wallenfang
Phenomenology by Donald Wallenfang
Virtue by Olli-Pekka Vainio
Reading Paul by Michael Gorman
The Rule of Faith by Everett Ferguson
The Second-Century Apologists by Alvyn Pettersen
Origen by Ronald E. Heine
Athanasius of Alexandria by Lois Farag
Practicing Lament by Rebekah Eklund
Forgiveness: A Theology by Anthony Bash
Called to Attraction: The Theology of Beauty by Brendan T. Sammon
A Primer in Ecotheology by Celia Deane-Drummond
Postmodern Theology by Carl Raschke
Jacques Ellul by Jacob E. Van Vleet and Jacob M. Rollinson
Understanding Pannenberg by Anthony C. Thiselton
The Becoming of God: Process Theology by Ronald Faber
Theology and Science Fiction by James F. McGrath
The U.S. Immigration Crisis by Miguel de la Torre
Feminism and Christianity by Caryn Riswold
Queer Theology by Linn Marie Tonstad

HAGGAI, ZECHARIAH, AND MALACHI

Hebrew Prophets of the Sixth and Fifth Centuries

JACK R. LUNDBOM

 CASCADE *Books* • Eugene, Oregon

HAGGAI, ZECHARIAH, AND MALACHI
Hebrew Prophets of the Sixth and Fifth Centuries

Cascade Companions

Copyright © 2025 Jack R. Lundbom. All rights reserved. Except for brief quotations in critical publications or reviews, no part of this book may be reproduced in any manner without prior written permission from the publisher. Write: Permissions, Wipf and Stock Publishers, 199 W. 8th Ave., Suite 3, Eugene, OR 97401.

Cascade Books
An Imprint of Wipf and Stock Publishers
199 W. 8th Ave., Suite 3
Eugene, OR 97401

www.wipfandstock.com

PAPERBACK ISBN: 979-8-3852-3738-8
HARDCOVER ISBN: 979-8-3852-3739-5
EBOOK ISBN: 979-8-3852-3740-1

Cataloguing-in-Publication data:

Names: Lundbom, Jack R., author.

Title: Haggai, Zechariah, and Malachi : Hebrew prophets of the sixth and fifth centuries / Jack R. Lundbom.

Description: Eugene, OR: Cascade Books, 2025. | Cascade Companions. | Includes bibliographical references and index.

Identifiers: ISBN 979-8-3852-3738-8 (paperback). | ISBN 979-8-3852-3739-5 (hardcover). | ISBN 979-8-3852-3740-1 (ebook).

Subjects: LCSH: Bible.—Haggai—Criticism, interpretation, etc. | Bible.—Zechariah—Criticism, interpretation, etc. | Bible.—Malachi—Criticism, interpretation, etc.

Classification: BS1665.53 2025 (print). | BS1665.53 (ebook).

06/27/25

Unless otherwise noted, Scripture translations are the author's.

To
Magnar Kartveit
in friendship

CONTENTS

Preface | xi
Abbreviations | xiii

1 Historical Survey of the Sixth and Fifth Centuries | 1
2 Prophets in the Sixth and Fifth Centuries | 9

HAGGAI

3 People Say: "It Is Not Time to Rebuild Yahweh's House" (1:1–2) | 37
4 You Have Sown Much, But Harvested Little (1:3–6) | 40
5 "Go Up to the Hills, Bring Wood and Build the House" (1:7–11) | 42
6 Work Begins on Yahweh's House (1:12–15) | 45
7 Who Is Left that Remembers Yahweh's Former House? (2:1–5) | 48
8 "The Latter Glory of This House Will Be Greater Than the Former" (2:6–9) | 51
9 Before and After the Foundation Was Laid (2:10–19) | 54
10 Zerubbabel to Be Yahweh's Chosen One (2:20–23) | 57

Contents

ZECHARIAH

11 Call to Repentance (1:1–6) | 61
12 Yahweh Is Returning to Jerusalem with Compassion (1:7–17) | 64
13 The Four Horns and Four Ironsmiths (1:18–21 [Heb. 2:1–4]) | 68
14 A Measuring Line for Jerusalem Not Needed (2:1–5 [Heb. 2:5–9]) | 70
15 Ho, Ho Zion! Escape Babylon (2:6–13 [Heb. 2:10–17]) | 72
16 I Will Bring My Servant, the Shoot (3:1–10) | 76
17 Zerubbabel Will Bring Forth the Top Stone Amid Shouts (4:1–14) | 80
18 The Flying Scroll (5:1–4) | 84
19 Wickedness in a Basket (5:5–11) | 86
20 The Four Chariots (6:1–8) | 89
21 Joshua Also Crowned the Shoot (6:9–15) | 92
22 Jerusalem to Be Called the Faithful City (8:1–8) | 96
23 Let Your Hands Be Strong! (8:9–13) | 99
24 Speak the Truth, Render True Judgments in the Gate! (8:14–17) | 102
25 Fasts and Feasts in Joy and Gladness (8:18–19) | 105
26 Many Will Seek Yahweh's Favor in Jerusalem (8:20–23) | 107

II. ZECHARIAH

27 Judgment against Syria, Phoenicia, and the Philistines (9:1–8) | 113
28 Messianic King Enters Zion in Triumph (9:9–17) | 117
29 In Yahweh's Name Shall People Walk About (10:3–12) | 122

Contents

30 Woe to the Worthless Shepherd! (11:4–17) | 127
31 Yahweh Will First Give Victory to Judah (12:7–14) | 132
32 A Fountain for the Cleansing of Jerusalem (13:1–6) | 136
33 A Day of Yahweh is Coming (14:1–21) | 139

MALACHI

34 Israel Unmindful of Yahweh's Love (1:2–5) | 147
35 Is Yahweh Pleased with Polluted Altar Food? (1:6—2:9) | 150
36 Yahweh Hates Divorce! (2:10–16) | 156
37 Yahweh's Messenger to Prepare the Way (2:17—3:12) | 160
38 A Book of Remembrance (3:13–18) | 165
39 The Day Is Coming (4:1–3 [Heb. 3:19–21]) | 168
40 I Will Send Elijah the Prophet (4:4–6 [Heb. 3:22–24]) | 170

Bibliography | 173

Name Index | 177

Scripture Index | 179

PREFACE

THIS BOOK SEEKS TO put before general readers background and selected preaching of Haggai, Zechariah, Malachi, and II Zechariah, four Hebrew prophets living in the sixth and fifth centuries B.C. Like other books in the Cascade Companions series, technical discussion and footnotes in this book are limited, leaving readers to consult commentaries and works in the bibliography for more information.

When nations and empires of the ancient world were destroyed, they left behind a legacy of great structures (Egypt), ruins of great structures (Greece and Rome), and recovered artifacts that today fill the museums of our world. Greece and Rome left behind an even greater legacy, e.g., written works in philosophy, medicine, drama, and rhetoric, some being recovered in the Christian High Middle Ages and again in the Renaissance of the fifteenth and sixteenth centuries. But when the tiny nation of Israel fell, a remnant of people, despite considerable adversity, lived on, following their God Yahweh (lit. He Will Be) during a Babylonian exile, a reestablishment under Persian rule in the Judahite homeland, and beyond. Jewish people continued to exist during the Greco-Roman period and survived a dispersion after AD 70 that sent them into all parts of the world—even China—only to emerge in the modern day when some have migrated back to the Holy Land to establish a state there. During the Babylonian exile and Persian rule this people was inspired, often chastised, by a succession of prophets. It is these prophets that the present book seeks to introduce to modern readers. Their prophecies are not well known; nevertheless, each has left his mark on the collective memory of Judaic and Christian communities. Haggai inspired people to get on with rebuilding the Temple. Zechariah supported him in the work and gave Messianic prophecies, pinning hopes on Zerubbabel, the Persian-appointed governor, and on Joshua the high priest. Both hopes went unfulfilled, but the prophecy found a later fulfillment in the life, death, and resurrection of Jesus the Christ. Malachi prophesied to a people in need of rebuke for its priests' offering polluted foods at Yahweh's altar and men divorcing their wives to marry foreign women. But Malachi gave Judahites a word of hope, promising a divine messenger who would prepare the way for the Messiah.

The Hebrew Masoretic Text used for translations of these prophets is that contained in the new *Biblia Hebraica Quinta (BHQ)* of The Twelve Minor Prophets, prepared by Anthony Gelston. All translations are my own.

I am pleased to dedicate this book to Magnar Kartveit, colleague and good friend of more than forty years. Dr. Kartveit has taught Old Testament at the School of Mission and Theology in Stavanger, Norway, specializing in postexilic Judaism with a particular interest in the community of Samaritans. He and his wife, Marit, are active members of the Lutheran Church in Norway. I have appreciated in Magnar a quiet strength, a commitment to teaching and research, and a devotion to both the church and the academy.

ABBREVIATIONS

AB	Anchor Bible
ABD	*Anchor Bible Dictionary*. Edited by David Noel Freedman. 6 vols. New York: Doubleday, 1992
ANE	ancient Near East
ANET	*Ancient Near Eastern Texts Relating to the Old Testament*. Edited by James B. Pritchard. 3rd ed. with Supplement. Princeton: Princeton University Press, 1969
ArBib	The Aramaic Bible
b.	Babylonian Talmud
BHK	*Biblia Hebraica*. Edited by Rudolf Kittel. 3rd ed. Leipzig: Hinrichs, 1937
BHQ	*Biblia Hebraica Quinta: The Twelve Minor Prophets*. Edited by Anthony Gelston. Stuttgart: Deutsche Bibelgesellschaft, 2010
BHS	*Biblia Hebraica Stuttgartensia*. Edited by Karl Elliger and Wilhelm Rudolph. 3rd ed. Stuttgart: Deutsche Bibelgesellschaft 1970
contra	Latin meaning "against"
CC	Continental Commentaries

Abbreviations

Gk.	Greek
Heb.	Hebrew
HTR	*Harvard Theological Review*
IBC	Interpretation: A Bible Commentary for Teaching and Preaching
ICC	The International Critical Commentary
Int	*Interpretation*
JNES	*Journal of Near Eastern Studies*
JSS	*Journal of Semitic Studies*
KJV	King James Version of the Bible
Kt	*kethib* (what is written)
LCL	Loeb Classical Library
lit.	literally
LXX	Greek Septuagint of the Hebrew Bible / Old Testament
MSS	manuscripts
MT	Masoretic Text of the Hebrew Bible / Old Testament
NICOT	New International Commentary on the Old Testament
NRSV	New Revised Standard Version of the Bible
NT	New Testament
OT	Old Testament
OTL	Old Testament Library
pace	Latin for "with due respect in opposition to"
Pesh	The Peshitta (Syriac) Bible
Qere	what is read
RSV	Revised Standard Version of the Bible

Abbreviations

TDOT	*Theological Dictionary of the Old Testament.* Edited by G. Johannes Botterweck, Helmer Ringgren, and Heinz-Josef Fabray. Translated by John T. Willis et al. 17 vols. Grand Rapids: Eerdmans, 1974–2021
Tg	Targum
Tiq soph	*tiqqune sopherim* (corrections of the scribes)
Vg	Vulgate
VT	*Vetus Testamentum*
WBC	Word Biblical Commentary

1

HISTORICAL SURVEY OF THE SIXTH AND FIFTH CENTURIES

THE SIXTH CENTURY BEGAN with Nebuchadnezzar and the Babylonian army poised to lay siege to Jerusalem. The army was continuing its military venture since destroying Nineveh and the Assyrian empire in 612 B.C. with help from the Medes, then crushing the Egyptians at the Battle of Carchemish (605), and going on to destroy Ashkelon and Ekron in the Philistine Plain (604–603). The full Babylonian army came to Jerusalem shortly after December 598, the month King Jehoiakim died. This wholly incompetent king was likely assassinated (cf. Jer 22:18–19). The Chronicler says he was bound to be taken to Babylon (2 Chr 36:6), but his death probably occurred before Nebuchadnezzar arrived in the city. Jehoiakim's eighteen-year-old son Jehoiachin was put on the throne, and three months later the city surrendered. Jehoiachin, the queen mother, officers, palace officials, and Jerusalem's skilled workers were deported to Babylon (2 Kgs 24; Jer 29:1–2). The number in Jer 52:28 is 3,023, but 8,000 in 2 Kgs 24:16. The king of Babylon put Zedekiah on the throne.

With most of Jerusalem's capable citizens gone, there was little over which to rule. Zedekiah's eleven years were marked by continual social and political unrest. Trouble on the southern front existed at the time. The Judahite fortress at Arad was destroyed in the third year of Zedekiah, apparently the work of the Edomites (Aharoni 1981: 40–41, 64). A rebellion in Babylon in 595 raised hopes both there and at home that Jehoiachin would return (Jer 27–28; 29:8–9, 21–23), but it was put down. Zedekiah's trip to Babylon in 594/3 (Jer 51:59) was probably to reaffirm his loyalty to Nebuchadnezzar (Bright 1981: 329).

By 589 Judah was rife with unrest. Zedekiah withheld tribute from Nebuchadnezzar (2 Kgs 24:20; Jer 52:3). In response the Babylonian army began another westward march, this time to put down resistance for good. The Lachish Letters corroborate the biblical account of Judah's last days (*ANET*, 321–22). Cities of Benjamin, e.g., Ramah and Mizpah, appear to have given up first (Malamat 1950: 226–27). Many other cities were destroyed at this time: Tell Beit Mirsim, Lachish, Gibeah, Ramat Raḥel, Arad, En-gedi, and others. The siege of Jerusalem was broken only briefly when Egypt made an advance, but that came to nothing. In the third year of the siege, now reckoned to be 586 (Tadmor 1956: 230), the wall of Jerusalem was breached and the city taken. A month later the Temple and the rest of the city was burned, with the Edomites lending a hand (Ezek 25:12; 35:5; Joel 3:19 [Heb. 4:19] and Ps 137:7; Obad 8–14). Another deportation to Babylon followed (832 persons according to Jer 52:29). Nationhood for Israel had come to an end.

Gedaliah, a grandson of Shaphan, was appointed governor over those who remained. Jeremiah, who had been given preferential treatment by the Babylonians, was placed with other refugees under Gedaliah's care at Mizpah. But then Gedaliah was murdered, which may have precipitated the third deportation of 745 persons in 581 (Jer 52:30). If so, the remnant community was in existence for about five years. The year 582 may have been when Jeremiah, Baruch, and the group to which they were attached left for Egypt. Jeremiah preached for a time to Jewish exiles in Egypt, warning them of, among other things, a future visit by Nebuchadnezzar to that nation with disastrous results (Jer 43:8–13). In 568 Nebuchadnezzar did invade Egypt (*ANET*, 308).

Back in Babylon, Nebuchadnezzar continued the massive building program begun by his father, Nabopolassar, making the city one of the wonders of the ancient world (Lundbom 2017). Nebuchadnezzar died in 562 and was succeeded by his son Amel-marduk, who reigned for just two years. Under him and his successors Babylonian power declined rapidly. Nevertheless, it was Amel-marduk, the Evil-merodach of the Bible, who released Jehoiachin from prison, giving the remnant community a glimmer of hope as noted in the closing words of the Deuteronomic History (2 Kgs 25:27–30). In 560 the throne was seized by Neriglissar, who is probably Nergal-sharezer, the Babylonian official, cited in Jer 39:3, 13 (Bright 1981: 352–53). He reigned for four years, and the throne was again seized by Nabonidus of Haran (556–539), who was the last king of Babylon. His reign was one of dissention and revolt, enough so that he transferred his residence to the oasis of Tema in the Arabian Desert, where he remained until his eleventh year (*ANET*, 306). Panic in Babylon during this time is reflected in Isa 41:1–7 and 46:1–2. Nabonidus returned to Babylon, but there faced a new power emerging to the east: Persia.

In 539 Cyrus and his army took Babylon without a fight, and by the next year the entire Babylonian Empire was under his control. The once-mighty Babylonian Empire had come to an end. Babylonian kings had ruled the Near Eastern world since the overthrow of Nineveh in 612, a total of seventy-three years. The round number of seventy years for Babylonian rule promised in Jer 25:11–12 and 29:10, then, was not far off.

In 538 Cyrus issued an edict allowing the Jews to return to Palestine and rebuild their Temple (2 Chr 36:22–23; Ezra 1:1–4; 6:1–5). Sacred Temple vessels taken to Babylon by Nebuchadnezzar were to be returned, a project given over to Sheshbazzar, "prince of Judah" (Ezra 1:7–11), who appears to be the Shenazzar mentioned in 1 Chr 3:18 as a son of Jehoiachin (Bright 1981: 361–62). By this year all western Asia to the Egyptian border was under Cryus's control. The Persian ruler showed a surprising benevolence toward the Babylonians as well as to other conquered peoples, in sharp contrast to the attitudes of Assyrian and Babylonian kings before him. Neither Babylon nor the outlying cities were harmed (*ANET*, 316). Cyrus allowed people to practice their own religions. His successors followed much the same policy. Cyrus is reported to have said, following his capture of Babylon:

> Therefore we dare not become careless nor give ourselves up to the enjoyment of the present moment; for, while I think it is a great thing to have won an empire, it is a still greater thing to preserve it after it has been won. For to win falls often to the lot of one who has shown nothing but daring; but to win and hold—that is no longer a possibility without the exercise of self-control, temperance, and unflagging care. (Xenophon *Cyropaedia* vii 76)

Historical Survey of the Sixth and Fifth Centuries

Cyrus died in battle and was succeeded by his son Cambyses (530–522), who five years later brought Egypt within the Persian Empire. During this time small groups of Jews returned to Palestine. Cambyses is said to have destroyed Egyptian temples (*ANET*, 492), but spared the temple of the Jewish community at Elephantine. We know very little about what was going on with the Jews in Palestine during this time. It was likely a "day of small things" (Zech 4:10). Albright (1963: 87, 110–11) estimates the Jewish population of Palestine in 522 to be about 20,000. Roughly seventy-five years later, when Nehemiah came to rebuild the walls of Jerusalem, the city remained largely a ruin (Neh 7:4).

When Cambyses died, Darius I became king (522–486). Darius was met with revolt throughout the empire, and only by 520 were rebellions put down. He went on to be a very able ruler, bringing Persian rule to its zenith. Also in 520 Zerubbabel, son of Jehoiachin's eldest son Shealtiel, succeeded his uncle Sheshbazzar as governor of Judah (Ezra 3:2, 8; cf. 1 Chr 3:17–19). The date of Zerubbabel's arrival in Judah is unknown, but he is believed to have come before 520 with a group of returning exiles. We know only that he was present in Darius's second year (Hag 1:1). Zerubbabel is credited with beginning the work of rebuilding the Temple, laying its foundation (Ezra 5:16). The high priest Joshua son of Jehozadak was also present in Jerusalem, directing spiritual affairs (Hag 1:1, 12, 14; cf. Ezra 3:2). Jehozadak, who went into Babylonian exile, was of Zadokite lineage (1 Chr 6:8–15 [Heb. 5:34–41]). Work on rebuilding the Temple began in 520, with Darius confirming the decree of Cyrus. The preaching of Haggai and Zechariah in the same year spurred the project on. Haggai and Zechariah hailed Zerubbabel as a Messianic figure (Hag 2:20–23; Zech 4:1–6, 10–14), a Davidic king promised for the future (Jer 23:5–6;

33:14–15). Four years later the Temple was completed and dedicated with great rejoicing (Ezra 5:1–2; 6:13–18).

Of the seventy years between the completion of the Temple and Nehemiah's appointment as governor of Judah in 445 we know almost nothing. Hopes of Haggai and Zechariah went unfulfilled, and Zerubbabel disappeared without a trace. Darius reigned until 486 and was succeeded by Xerxes I (486–465). Xerxes captured Athens but was defeated elsewhere in Greece. All that was said of this king (misnamed Ahasuerus) in Ezra 4:6 is that during his time the Samaritans spoke ill of the Jews to the Persian court. In 465 Xerxes was assassinated and succeeded by his son Artaxerxes I, who reigned from 465 to 424. During his reign Ezra and Nehemiah came to Palestine, work began on rebuilding Jerusalem's walls, and both men undertook a thorough reorganization of the Jewish community. These years also saw the beginning of the golden age in Greece, of Pericles, Socrates, Sophocles, and others.

In 458, which was the seventh year of Artaxerxes I, Ezra had been granted permission to go to Jerusalem with a large company (Ezra 7:1—8:36).[1] The journey took four months (Ezra 7:8–9). After arriving, he read the Torah to people in Jerusalem with Levites translating the Hebrew into Aramaic and giving an interpretation. It was a deeply moving event, with people weeping as they heard words of the Torah. The autumn Feast of Booths was then celebrated (Neh 8). Malachi was preaching in Jerusalem by the midfifth century.

Then in 445 Nehemiah, cupbearer to Artaxerxes, after making a plea to the Persian king, was given permission to begin rebuilding the walls of Jerusalem (Neh 2:1–8). He was subsequently appointed governor of Judah (Neh 5:14; 10:1).

---

1. So Williamson (1985: xliv); Bright (1981: 386) dates Ezra's arrival to 428.

Historical Survey of the Sixth and Fifth Centuries

By 440 Nehemiah was in Jerusalem beginning the work. A wall of sorts was up in fifty-two days (Neh 6:15), despite opposition from Sanballat, governor of Samaria (Neh 4:1–2). Josephus (*Ant* xi 179), however, says actual completion of the wall required two years and four months.

Nehemiah remained in Jerusalem twelve years, until 433 (Neh 5:14), when he returned to the Persian court. Soon after, however, he petitioned the king to return to Jerusalem where he found Tobiah, his enemy, in possession of a room in the Temple. He proceeded to toss Tobiah's furniture out of the room and cleanse the Temple chambers (Neh 13:4–9).[2]

By the fifth century B.C. Jews were well established in various parts of the empire. There was a Jewish community as far away as Sardis in Asia Minor, sixty miles east of Ephesus, as well as in Lower Egypt (Isa 19:16–25). A Jewish colony at Elephantine in the First Cataract of the Nile was in existence throughout the fifth century. It had a temple to Yahweh and a syncretistic form of Yahwistic worship, with other divinities also worshiped by Jews living there. Back in Palestine the Edomites, who had been displaced in their homeland by Arab tribes (Mal 1:2–5), occupied most of southern Palestine.

In 424 Artaxerxes I, who had been Nehemiah's patron, died and was succeeded by Xerxes II (423), then Darius II (423–404). Artaxerxes II (404–358) became king of Persia at the death of Darius II. Persia intervened at this time in support of Sparta, ending the Peloponnesian War. In the late Persian period (404–333) we have another period in which almost nothing is known about fortunes of the Jewish people—whether in Babylon, Judah and elsewhere in the Persian Empire, or in Lower Egypt. The biblical narrative stops, and

---

2. Over in Greece, the Peloponnesian War between Athens and Sparta broke out in 431, lasting until 404.

the Elephantine texts break off as the fourth century begins (*ANET*, 491–92). At this time the Samaritans probably built their own temple on Mount Gerizim (Bright 1981: 410).

REFLECTION

1. Why do you think Nebuchadnezzar took skilled workers from Jerusalem into exile in 598 (Jer 29:2)?

2. Cyrus and the Persians were benevolent toward the peoples they conquered, unlike the Assyrians and Babylonians. Do some nations today act more benevolently than others toward the people they conquer? What about America's General MacArthur, who proved to be the great peacemaker in a defeated Japan? And what about America's Marshall Plan that rebuilt Europe after World War II?

2

PROPHETS IN THE SIXTH AND FIFTH CENTURIES

THE TWELVE PROPHETS

THE HEBREW BIBLE CONTAINS the so-called Book of the Twelve consisting of Hosea, Joel, Amos, Obadiah, Jonah, Micah, Nahum, Habakkuk, Zephaniah, Haggai, Zechariah, and Malachi, referred to also as the Minor Prophets, a title first appearing in Augustine (*De civitate dei* xviii, 29).[1] Augustine referred to the small size of these works when compared with Isaiah, Jeremiah, and Ezekiel, who were the Major Prophets. Twelve prophets are referred to in Sir 49:10 where it says they comforted people and gave them hope. Their prophecies were probably written on a single scroll at the time Sirach was written, i.e., 180 B.C. Haggai, Zechariah, and Malachi were the last of the prophets; with

---

1. Eissfeldt, *Old Testaments*, 383.

them prophecy was said to have ended in ancient Israel. The Talmud says: "When Haggai, Zechariah, and Malachi died, the Holy Spirit departed from Israel" (b. Sota 48b; cf. 1 Macc 9:27).

WHAT MANNER OF INDIVIDUAL IS THE PROPHET?

Consciousness of Inspiration

Abraham Joshua Heschel (1962: 426–27) says prophets were conscious of being inspired, where Haggai among others is cited:

> The certainty of being inspired by God, of speaking in his name, of having been sent by Him to the people, is the basic and central fact of the prophet's consciousness . . . The prophet does not speak of a resolution or a purpose, framed by himself, to devote himself to his vocation, but describes a decisive moment in which he received a call. He thinks of himself as a "man of God" (Hag 1:13), sent by Him to His people (Jer 26:12–14; Isa 49:5–6).

Yahweh's Attachment to Zion

Heschel (1962: 95–96) notes how later Hebrew prophets held to ideas of their predecessors. Isaiah, unlike Jeremiah, never predicted the destruction of Jerusalem. For this prophet God had a "lasting, indestructible attachment to His people and to Zion." Zechariah says later: "For thus said the Lord of hosts, after his glory sent me to the nations who plundered you, for he who touches you touches the apple of his eye" (Zech 2:8; [Heb. 2:12]). "Zion is where at the end of days all the nations shall go to learn the ways of God" (Zech 2).

Yahweh Is Also God of His Enemies

Heschel (1962: 185–86) says "the God of Israel is also the God of his enemies, without their knowing Him and despite their defying him. Enmity between nations will turn into friendship; they will live together when they worship together." He cites the visionary prophet of the exile who says, "My house shall be called a house of prayer for all peoples" (Isa 56:7b). Zechariah, too, says, "Many nations shall join themselves to the Lord in that day, and shall be My people" (Zech 2:11 [Heb. 2:15]).

The Highest Good

Heschel (1962: 7–9) says "three things ancient society cherished above all else: wisdom, wealth, and might." The prophet lifts up something else. Jeremiah says, "Let not the wise man glory in his wisdom, let not the mighty man glory in his might, let not the rich man glory in his riches; but let him who glories, glory in this, that he understands and knows Me, that I am the Lord Who practices kindness, justice, and righteousness in the earth; for in these things I delight, says the Lord" (Jer 9:23–24 [Heb. 9:22–23]). Zechariah's expression is much the same, but with astounding finality: "This is the word of the Lord . . . : Not by might, nor by power, but by My spirit" (Zech 4:6).

A Unity of History

Heschel (1962: 169–70) says we see in the Hebrew prophets "a unity of history" that parallels the Israelite view of the unity of God. The prophet "is concerned with, and addresses himself to, all men" (Amos 1:3—2:6; Isa 14:24–27; Jer 1:5; 28:8). Malachi cites the unity of God as bearing upon the required unity of one to another: "Have we not all one father? Has not one God created us? Why then are we faithless to one another, profaning the covenant of our fathers?" (Mal 2:10).

Prophecy and Divination

Heschel (1962: 457–58, 461) says "the biblical attitude to Semitic divination was one of uncompromising antagonism; its practice being universally forbidden." "The contrast between prophecy and divination was stressed in the book of Deuteronomy: 'For these nations . . . give heed to soothsayers and to diviners; but as for you, the Lord your God has not allowed you to do so. The Lord your God will raise up for you a prophet like me.'" (Deut 18:14–15). Jeremiah, Ezekiel, and II Zechariah equate diviners with falseness or false prophets (Jer 14:14; 27:9–10; 29:8; Ezek 13:1–9; Zech 10:2). Jeremiah "drew a sharp distinction between a prophet who had the word of God and him who had 'a dream.'" (Jer 23:28–32), dreamers being put on par with diviners, soothsayers, and sorcerers (Jer 27:9). II Zechariah says much the same:

> For the teraphim utter nonsense,
> The diviners see lies;
> The dreamers tell false dreams,
> And give empty consolations.
> Therefore the people wander like sheep;
> They are afflicted for want of a shepherd.
> (Zech 10:2)

HAGGAI

Although the book of Haggai lacks a superscription like that found in most prophetic books, we know about this prophet only from what is written in the book bearing his name and from the mention of him with Zechariah in Ezra 5:1 and 6:14. Haggai is not mentioned in the list of returning exiles in Ezra 2 and Neh 7, nor does his book mention any recollection of the exile, as Zechariah does (cf. Zech 1:14–17; 2:6–12 [Heb. 2:10–16]; 6:15). Hans Walter Wolff suggests that because of a lively interest in farming problems in his home country (1:6, 10–11; 2:16, 19), Haggai may have belonged to country folk who had remained in Palestine. But we do not know if this is the case. Haggai's prophecies are dated during three and a half months in the year 520.

The book of Haggai begins with a word from Yahweh stating a belief circulating among the people, viz., that it is not time to rebuild the Temple (1:1–2). Haggai's entire prophecy argues to the contrary. He asks the people—or perhaps Zerubbabel and Joshua, leaders of the community—if it is time for them to live in paneled houses while Yahweh's house lies in ruins? He points out that people have sown much but harvested little. Perhaps a reason exists for the poor harvests! (1:3–6). In a second oracle the prophet tells people to go up to the hills, get wood, and get on with building Yahweh's house so it may be glorified. Yahweh has brought the drought and withheld the grain, wine, and oil, affecting both humans and animals (1:7–11).

We learn then that people heeded the words of Haggai and feared Yahweh, with the result that the work of rebuilding began (1:12–15). In his next oracle Haggai asks, Who among the remnant community remembers the glory of the former Temple, and how do they see it now? It is a pile of rubble! Nevertheless, Zerubbabel, Joshua, and all the people are told to be strong, for Yahweh is with them as he was when Israel was delivered out of Egypt (2:1–5). In a subsequent oracle Haggai tells people that the latter glory of Yahweh's house will be greater than the former, for the wealth of the nations will be brought to it. Yahweh will also give peace to the place (2:6–9).

Haggai in the next oracle reminds people how they fared before the new Temple's foundation was laid, when the yield of grain and wine was meager. It was because Yahweh struck the land with blight, mildew, and hail, and people did not come to him. But from this day forward, since the foundation of the Temple has been laid, yield has been plentiful (2:10–19). Haggai's final prophecy is Messianic: Nations are soon to be destroyed; Zerubbabel is announced as Yahweh's chosen one and given his signet ring (2:20–23).

ZECHARIAH

Zechariah prophesied in the second and fourth years of Darius I (i.e., in 520 and 518 [Zech 1:1, 7; 7:1]), being a contemporary of Haggai and cooperating with him in efforts to rebuild the Temple (Ezra 5:1–2; 6:14). A (grand)son of Iddo, he is identified with Iddo the priest in Neh 12:4, which means like Jeremiah and Ezekiel he was both prophet and priest. A tradition survives in the Targum to Lam 2:20, repeated in Matt 23:35, that Zechariah was martyred. Zechariah today is only credited with prophecies in chapters 1–8 of his book. Prophecies in chapters 9–14 are thought to emanate from an unknown prophet in the later Persian age.

Zechariah's prophecies fall into two parts: (1) eight visions of hope and encouragement for Judahites (1:7—6:8) preceded by a call to repentance and an act of repentance (1:1–6) and followed by an oracle on "the Shoot" (6:9–15);

and (2) Yahweh's promises and moral demands for the future.

Yahweh was very angry with the people's ancestors. He called them to return, i.e., repent, but they paid no heed, so his word overtook them. Then they repented, realizing that Yahweh did to them exactly what he said he would do (1:1–6).

In Zechariah's first vision the prophet sees four horsemen Yahweh has sent to patrol the earth, and they report that all the land is quiet. Yahweh is jealous for Jerusalem and for Zion, very jealous. He was only a little angry with his people; his anger is now against nations who are at ease. Yahweh will return to Jerusalem, and his house will be rebuilt. A measuring line will be stretched out over Jerusalem and Judah's cities will again overflow with prosperity. Yahweh will comfort Zion and again choose Jerusalem as his city (1:7–17).

A second vision is of four iron horns and four ironsmiths. The four horns are nations that scattered Judah, Israel, and Jerusalem so that no one could lift up his head. The four smiths have come to terrify these nations and strike them down (1:18–21 [Heb. 2:1–4]).

The third vision is of a young man with a measuring line in hand, coming to measure Jerusalem. But someone runs to tell him that a measuring line will be unnecessary because the city will be without walls, so many people and cattle will be residing within her. Yahweh will be a wall of fire around Jerusalem and be the glory within her (2:1–5 [Heb. 2:5–9]).

2:6–13 [Heb. 2:10–17] is an epilogue to the third vision. In excited tones the prophet tells Judahites still in Babylon to escape and return to Jerusalem. Yahweh is about to rain judgment on the nations, who will become plunder for those who served them, especially Judahites. Daughter Zion is told to sing and rejoice, for Yahweh is coming to dwell in her midst. What is more, peoples from many nations will join Israel in the worship of Yahweh in the Jerusalem Temple, where they, too, will be Yahweh's people. Zechariah says: Be in silent awe, for Yahweh is ready to move from his holy habitation.

The fourth vision begins with Yahweh cleansing Joshua the high priest and all Judahites for prior sins, announcing thereafter that he is bringing forth his servant, the Shoot (3:1–10). The high priest is on trial in a (heavenly) court of law where Joshua is standing before an angel of Yahweh with the Satan at his right ready to accuse the priest. But Yahweh rebukes the Satan. Has not Jerusalem, whom the high priest represents, been as a brand plucked out of the fire? We find out why the Satan was ready to accuse: Joshua is clothed in filthy garments, representing the prior sins of the nation of Judah. Nevertheless, the Satan is silenced. The angel of Yahweh calls for the removal of the filthy garments from off him; his iniquity has been taken away and he is to be dressed in stately robes. A clean turban is to be put on his head. The angel then solemnly enjoins Joshua that if he walks in Yahweh's way and keeps Yahweh's charge, he will rule in Yahweh's house and give right of entry to those standing by. Joshua is further told that he and fellow Zadokite priests sitting before him will see Yahweh bringing forth his servant, the Shoot, who in all probability is Zerubbabel. The stone set before Joshua is a top stone for the Temple. The day will be a happy one, for everyone will invite his fellow to sit under his vine and under his fig tree.

The fifth vision is of a gold lampstand with seven lamps flanked by two olive trees (4:1–14). The angel speaking to Zechariah says: "This is the word of Yahweh to Zerubbabel: Not by might, and not by power, but with my Spirit." Before Zerubbabel a great mountain will become a plain, and he will bring the top stone of the Temple amid shouts: "Grace,

grace to it." Zerubbabel laid the foundation of the Temple, and he will finish it. Yahweh's watchful eyes remain over the work. The olive trees on either side of the lampstand are the two "sons of oil" who stand by the Lord of the whole earth, viz., Joshua the high priest and Zerubbabel the governor.

The sixth vision is of a large flying scroll, twenty cubits in length and ten cubits in width. When Zechariah asks what is written on the scroll, he is told it contains curses for everyone who steals and swears falsely. Yahweh will send the scroll into the house of the thief and the perjurer where it will consume the house timber and stones (5:1–4).

The seventh vision is of Wickedness in a basket (5:5–11). Zechariah sees a basket of ephah quantity coming forth. It had a lid, and when the round cover of lead is lifted, behold! a woman is sitting there. The prophet is told, "This is Wickedness" existing throughout the land. The woman is then cast down and the cover replaced over the basket. The prophet then sees two other women with wings like a stork who lift the basket between earth and heaven. He asks where they are taking the basket, and is told it is going to Shinar (Babylon) where a house will be built for it, and it will rest there on its base.

The eighth vision in 6:1–8 is of four chariots drawn by horses of four colors, hearkening back to the men on four horses of color in the first vision (1:7–17). In both visions the horsemen are out patrolling the earth. The chariots here are going forth from between two mountains of bronze, headed in different directions. The chariots with black horses are headed to the north country where Yahweh's wrathful spirit is said to be "quieted" (i.e., it is being poured forth upon Babylon).

The concluding passage in the first section of Zechariah features a symbolic act by the prophet (6:9–15). Joshua the high priest is now crowned as "the Shoot." In the fourth vision his filthy garments were removed, and he was given stately robes, and a clean turban was placed on his head (3:1–10). But there the "Shoot" was to be Zerubbabel. Here three individuals, Heldai, Tobijah, and Jedaiah, recent returnees from Babylon, have brought with them some of their wealth and are taken into the house of Josiah (probably a metalworker) to have silver and gold crowns made. One crown is to be set on the head of Joshua, and he is to be named "the Shoot." The three men just introduced act as witnesses. Joshua will have a role in rebuilding the Temple and will rule as priest upon his throne. Peaceful relations will exist between him and Zerubbabel. The crowns will then be placed as a memorial in the Temple. Other exiles will come to help in the rebuilding project, but this will happen only if people diligently obey the voice of Yahweh their God.

Part II of the book of Zechariah (chapters 7–8) consists of a series of oracles with promises from Yahweh and moral demands for the people. In the first passage (7:1–7), returned exiles living in Bethel send two individuals, Sharezer and Regem-melech, to Jerusalem to entreat Yahweh's favor and inquire of the priests and the prophets whether they should continue mourning and fasting as they have done for many years. Zechariah gives them this word from Yahweh: Did they fast and mourn in prior years for him? Did they not eat and drink only for themselves? That's what the former prophets told them when Jerusalem and the surrounding territory was inhabited and enjoying prosperity.

In the next passage people are told to execute true judgments in the city gates, also to show steadfast love and mercy toward one another. They are not to oppress the widow, the orphan, the sojourner, or the poor, nor are they to devise evil one against another. Earlier generations refused to heed these teachings of Deuteronomy or to listen to former prophets whom Yahweh sent. So, Yahweh in great wrath whirled them like a storm wind to nations they had not known, and the pleasant land they inherited from Yahweh became desolate with no one passing through (7:8–14).

In 8:1–8 Yahweh says he is jealous for Zion with a great jealousy; this jealousy for her means great wrath toward her enemies. Yahweh is returning to Zion. Jerusalem will be called the faithful city, and Mount Zion will be Yahweh's holy mountain. In this future day old men and old women, with staffs in hand, will be seen sitting in the streets, and around them boys and girls will be playing. If it will be marvelous in the eyes of this remnant people, will it not also be marvelous in the eyes of Yahweh? Yahweh says he will save people from east and west, bringing them to Jerusalem where they will be his people and he will be their God—in faithfulness and in righteousness.

In the next oracle (8:9–13) Yahweh tells people: Let your hands be strong, those of you who have heard this day words from the prophets (i.e., from Haggai and Zechariah), which came when the foundation of the Temple was laid, that it might be fully built up. In former days no wages were paid for human or animal work, nor was there peace from the foe; further, internal dissention existed: Yahweh set everyone against his fellow. But now, not as in former days, the seed of peace will be sown, the vine will yield its fruit, the earth will give its increase, and the heavens will give their dew. The remnant people will possess all these things. Formerly they were a curse among the nations, but now Yahweh will save them and make them a blessing. Do not fear! Let your hands be strong!

The next oracle is another admonition to speak the truth and render true judgments in the city gates (8:14–17). Yahweh says, just as he purposed to do evil when their ancestors provoked him to wrath, and he did not relent, so now he has purposed to do good to Jerusalem and the house of Judah. Do not fear! But these are the things people must do: speak the truth, each to his fellow; render true and peaceful judgments in the gates; do not devise evil in the heart one against the other; and do not love a false oath. All these things Yahweh hates.

In the next brief oracle Yahweh tells the prophet to see that people make all their fasts and pilgrim feasts times of joy and gladness. People are to love truth and peace.

Zechariah concludes his words of hope and prosperity and his demands for the remnant community by first repeating the oft-stated theme that people from all nations will come to Jerusalem to worship Yahweh. There will be a sense of urgency in those days. One will say to another, "Let me go also!" More than that, ten men, speaking every language, will grab hold of the corner of each Judahite's skirt, saying, "Let us go with you, for we have heard that God is with you."

II ZECHARIAH

Second Zechariah is the name given to the prophet (or prophets) responsible for prophecies in chapters 9–14 of the book of Zechariah. This biblical book has combined later prophecies with words from a known prophet, just as the book of Isaiah has. Earlier Jewish and Christian writers took the entire book (i.e., chapters 1–14) to be from the historical Zechariah (Mitchell: 232), but with the rise of critical scholarship important differences were noted between chapters 1–8 and 9–14. Zechariah, like Haggai, has dated prophecies, whereas II Zechariah's prophecies contain no dates, nor does the latter contain any reference to known persons or events. In Zechariah the prophet speaks in the first person, whereas II Zechariah has no first-person speech except in 11:4-16. Zechariah also contains visions, whereas II Zechariah has none, having as it does prophetic oracles of the more classical sort (Mitchell: 233; Boda: 26). Zech 9:1-8 indicts foreign nations as do earlier prophets. The literary form of Zechariah is also different from the literary form of II Zechariah (Mitchell: 234-235; Petersen: 24).

Early critical scholars dated II Zechariah to the Greek period, in part because of a reference to Greece in 9:13. 9:1-10 was said to date from Alexander's defeat of Darius III at Issus in 333 (Mitchell: 252-53, 258), and 9:11—11:3 from the reign of Ptolemy III (247-222). Alexander was known to be friendly to the Jews (Mitchell: 254-55). More recently, however, Zech 9-14 has been dated to the Persian period. Achtemeier (146) says: "As to those who added chapters 9-14 to Zechariah 1-8 and when, there is no reason to assign them to a period other than the last half of the sixth century B.C." Battles in 9:1-17 are not historical battles, but the final battle preceding the coming of the kingdom to Jerusalem. "Greece" in 9:13 is a symbol "for unknown peoples on the edge of civilization" (Achtemeier: 147). Petersen also sees the Persian period as background for 9-14, as does Boda, who prefers the early Persian period. Boda dates core material in 9-10 to ca. 515-510, reflecting the period after the dedication of the Temple in 515; 11:4-16 reflects the events surrounding the end of Zerubbabel's reign (ca. 510); and the oracular material in 12-14 is dated during the period of Nehemiah's governorship in 445-433. The book in its final form is addressed to those living in the mid- to late fifth century (Boda: 33-37, 521). Boda: 28 also argues that chapters 1-14 should be treated as a single book.

I line up with those dating II Zechariah to the Persian period. I also believe its author is someone consciously preaching in Zechariah's name. In 12:10 the prophet, in a surprising use of the first-person pronoun (MT), assumes he is Zechariah, whom tradition says was martyred. The prophet cannot be referring to himself as someone already dead. Jesus in the NT says Zechariah son of Barachiah was murdered between the sanctuary and the altar (Matt 23:35; cf. Zech 1:1).

Second Zechariah divides in two: a first oracle comprising chapters 9–11, and a second oracle comprising chapters 12–14. 9:1–8 announces Yahweh's judgment upon Syria, Phoenicia, and the Philistines, their depopulated territory being incorporated into Judah. But from the half-breed people inhabiting Ashdod Yahweh will take the idolatrous sacrifices out of their mouths. From the mongrel people inhabiting Philistia will also come a remnant that will worship Yahweh and be incorporated into Judah. Yahweh in this day will protect his land, especially Jerusalem.

In 9:9–17 the Messianic King enters Zion in triumph. He is righteous and victorious, humble and riding on a donkey. Horses and chariots will be cut off from North Israel and Jerusalem, and this king will speak peace to the nations. Northern Israel will be occupied by its former inhabitants. Addressing exiles still in Babylon, Yahweh says he will set them free from their captivity, and they are encouraged to return to Zion where they will be remunerated in kind. Yahweh then shifts to talk about warfare. He will make a dramatic victory over the Greeks. The covenant people will greatly rejoice, being now as crown jewels on Yahweh's land.

In the next passage people are told to ask Yahweh for rain (10:1–2). It is Yahweh, after all, who brings rain, not the teraphim, diviners, and dreamers, who, because of their lies leave people wandering about like sheep without a shepherd.

Prophets in the Sixth and Fifth Centuries

In 10:3–12 Yahweh says he will visit foreign rulers to punish, but his own people he will visit to deliver from oppression. Yahweh will be with his people in the fight. Exiles still in Assyria and Babylon will be brought home, and Yahweh will have compassion on them. Their children will be glad. So many will be the returnees that there will not be enough room for them. Reference is made to Israel's earlier deliverance at the Red Sea. In this future day people will walk about in Yahweh's name.

11:1–3 is a brief passage of uncertain meaning. It appears foreign rulers are to be brought down, with Judahite rulers beholden to them suffering the same fate. "Zerubbabel and/or his descendants may have entered into inappropriate liaisons with foreign imperial authorities" (Boda: 645).

Verses 4–17 declare woe on worthless shepherds people have allowed to rule them. The passage is a symbolic act laden with irony. Yahweh tells the prophet to shepherd a flock readied for market. Current buyers have been killing sheep and are not held guilty; current sellers bless Yahweh because they have become rich. The current buyers and sellers are probably Judahite leaders. Because of poor leadership, Yahweh will no longer have pity on his people. The consequences will be enormous. People will fight with one another and also with their king, and Yahweh will not deliver any of the victims.

The prophet then assumes his task of shepherding the doomed flock. He has two staffs in hand, one called Pleasant and the other called Bind. In one month he destroys three of the worthless shepherds. Finally, he becomes impatient with them, and they with him, so he leaves the sheep to their fate. The staff named Pleasant is broken, annulling the covenant of peace made between Yahweh and the people. The poor flock witnessing all this knew it was the word of Yahweh.

The prophet then asks his fellow Judahites for his wages, in 11:12–14, not knowing if they will be paid. Well, they are paid, a paltry thirty shekels of silver. Disgusted with the sum, he throws it to the potter in the Temple, after which he breaks his second staff, Bind, breaking the family ties between Israel and Judah. In a supplement Yahweh tells the prophet to again assume the implements of a worthless shepherd. It is now to be a sign that Yahweh is raising up a shepherd who will look after his people. The supplement closes with a declaration of woe on the worthless shepherd.

The second oracle of II Zechariah opens with a word concerning Israel, especially Jerusalem (12:1–6). The God who created heaven and earth, forming also the human spirit, says he is about to make Jerusalem a bowl of reeling to all peoples round about. These are perhaps the Ammonites, Moabites, and Edomites, and even Judah, who have assembled to besiege Jerusalem. The bowl is probably filled with wine. But besieging the city (that is, drinking from the bowl) will be a burden heavier than any can undertake without incurring serious loss. Yahweh will strike every fighter and his horse with madness and blindness. But then he will open his eyes upon Judah when foes are attacking Jerusalem, causing Judah in turn to recognize that Jerusalem has strength through Yahweh its God. Clans of Judah will then turn against their assailants, who will be like destructive fires to them on the right and on the left, with the result that Jerusalem will remain in its place.

12:7–14 follows with Yahweh saying he will first give victory to Judah so Jerusalem, who boasts as being the city of David, will not exalt itself over the rest of Judah. But he is quick to add that he will nevertheless defend the inhabitants of Jerusalem. Yahweh in that day will destroy all nations coming against Jerusalem. He will pour out upon the house of David and Jerusalem a spirit of grace and supplication so they will request forgiveness for sins committed. And people will look upon (Zechariah) whom they have pierced and mourn bitterly for him. The entire land will mourn, families in succession, and women separately.

In 13:1–6 we hear of a fountain being opened for those of Davidic lineage and the rest of Jerusalem's population to cleanse themselves from sin and uncleanness. Their sin is idols and the prophets who prophesy by them. Yahweh will cut off both from the land. Parents of pretending prophets must put them to death. Pretending prophets are to deny that they are prophets and not dress up as prophets.

The brief poetry in 13:7–9 describes the fate of Yahweh's foolish shepherd and his flock, about which more was said in 11:4–17. This shepherd will be smitten, and only one-third of the flock will survive, after fiery trials, to be Yahweh's covenant people. The prophecy concludes with the Sinai covenant formula.

The concluding passage in II Zechariah describes a future day of Yahweh in which Jerusalem will first be assaulted by nations, the city taken, and its spoil divided among the attackers. Half of the city will go into exile. But then Yahweh will appear standing on the Mount of Olives and will fight against those nations. The Mount will be rent in two, and those remaining in the city will escape into a great valley created between the divided mountain. Yahweh will be attended by all his holy ones. The Messianic Age will commence. Day and night will be no more, and a perennial stream of water will flow out of Jerusalem. Yahweh will be King over all the earth and be worshiped by all as one God with one name.

The territory of Judah will then sink and become like the Arabah, but Jerusalem will remain in its place. City inhabitants will dwell in security and no longer go into exile. The ban against holy war will be no more. In this future day

Yahweh will destroy the nations that have warred against Jerusalem. A plague will descend upon both humans and beasts, and Jerusalem's enemies will slay one another in the confusion. In this day Jerusalem will gain immense wealth from the nations. Those surviving the onslaught against the nations will become worshipers of Yahweh and make the yearly pilgrimage to the Feast of Booths in Jerusalem. Drought and plague await any nation that does not go up. Yahweh's crowning act will be to establish the holiness of Jerusalem. Horses will have bells since they too will be holy to Yahweh. All Temple vessels will be declared holy, and no trader will enter Yahweh's house in those days.

MALACHI

Malachi is the last canonical book of the OT. It may name a prophet whose prophecies are contained in the book, or be the anonymous work of one identified with "my messenger" (Heb. *mal'ākî*) in 3:1. The superscription of the LXX has "by the hand of his messenger" (ἐν χειρὶ ἀγγέλου). The Targum names the messenger as Ezra the scribe. The precise date of Malachi's prophecies is unknown. They are usually placed in the mid-fifth century, before Ezra came to Jerusalem and carried out his religious reform, and before Nehemiah came to carry out his responsibilities as governor and initiate the rebuilding of Jerusalem's walls. One reason for placing the prophecies before Nehemiah became governor is that in 1:8 the prophet suggests to priests that they try presenting inferior gifts to the governor, who would have to be a governor prior to Nehemiah since Nehemiah says he took no gifts (Neh 5:14–18).

Malachi is speaking to a dispirited community of returned exiles. The glories of II Isaiah had given way to harsher realities, and Messianic hopes in the time of Haggai and Zechariah had come to nothing. Troubles came from Samaritans up north. The priesthood was corrupt, and people did not see the hand of God in anything taking place. Malachi's first word has Yahweh contrasting the lots of Israel and Edom, saying he has loved Israel and made Edom's land a permanent desolation (1:2–5).

A second passage censures the priesthood for bringing blind, lame, sick, and stolen animals to sacrifice on Yahweh's altar, thinking it is no harm to do so (1:6—2:9). But Yahweh does not accept such sacrifices. He is a great King, and his name is revered among the nations. The priests are told if they will not lay this matter to heart they will be cursed, their seed will be rebuked, and Yahweh will disgrace them with dung from the animals they sacrifice. Yahweh gave Levi a covenant of life and peace, and unless these priests amend their ways they will be despised and abased before all the people.

In 2:10–16 Malachi rebukes Judahites who have divorced the wives of their youth to marry foreign women. Yahweh hates these divorces. Israel has one Father, and these individuals have profaned Yahweh's sanctuary by marrying daughters of a foreign god. They want to know why Yahweh has not accepted their offerings. Answer: Because they have mistreated and divorced their wives. May Yahweh cut off anyone doing this from the Judahite community and from bringing an offering to Yahweh. Divorces are faithless acts. Malachi closes by calling individuals to give heed to their (inner) spirit and not to be faithless.

In 2:17—3:12 people in the restored community are said to have wearied Yahweh with their claim that Yahweh delights in evildoers, and they ask, "Where is the God of justice?" Yahweh has a ready answer. He is sending his messenger to prepare the way for his sudden appearance in the Temple. It will be a day of judgment, however, and who can endure it? Yahweh's purpose is to refine and cleanse sons of Levi until they present offerings to him in righteousness. Then their offerings will be pleasing as in former days. Yahweh will be a swift witness against sorcerers, adulterers, and perjurers; also against those oppressing hired workers, widows, and orphans; and opposed to those mistreating resident aliens. Such people do not revere Yahweh.

Yahweh issues a call for return, which is a call for repentance. In what way? By not robbing God in the presentation of tithes and offerings. People are to bring the full tithe into the storehouse and see if Yahweh will not rain down a more than sufficient blessing. It will be seen in the vines and field crops. All nations will count Israel happy for it will be a land of delight.

In 3:13–18 Yahweh says that people have spoken harsh words against him. How so? They say it profits not to serve Yahweh or walk about in mourning clothes. The arrogant are counted happy; evildoers not only prosper, but when they put God to the test they escape. But then a small company of pious folk who revere Yahweh speak with one another, and Yahweh listens. Being pleased with what he hears, Yahweh has a book of remembrance written of those who revere him, saying he will make them a treasure piece on the day he comes, and will spare them. On that day all doubters will return and discern between the righteous and the wicked, between one who serves Yahweh and one who does not.

In 4:1–3 [Heb. 3:19–21] Yahweh speaks of a coming day when the arrogant and evildoers will be burned as stubble while those revering his name will be warmed by the sun of righteousness with healing in its wings. The latter will go out in joy, like calves leaping from the stall. They will tread down the wicked, who will become ashes under their feet.

In a final prophecy people are admonished to remember the statutes and ordinances taught by Moses. Yahweh will send the prophet Elijah before his great and terrible day, and he will turn the heart of fathers to their children and the heart of children to their fathers, lest he come and strike the land with a curse.

TIMELINE OF THE SIXTH AND FIFTH CENTURIES

Jeremiah

598 In December, Nebuchadnezzar and the full Babylonian army arrive in Jerusalem.

Jehoiakim is dead; likely assassinated. Young King Jehoiachin, the queen mother, palace officials, and skilled workers are deported to Babylon. Ezekiel is among those exiled.

Ezekiel

595 Ezekiel the priest is called to be a prophet in Babylon.

586 Jerusalem and Judah fall to Nebuchadnezzar and the Babylonians. A remnant community is established at Mizpah.

Obadiah

582 Jeremiah and Baruch are taken with a group to Egypt.

581 A Babylonian official returns to Jerusalem after Gedeliah's murder at Mizpah, and another group is taken into Babylonian exile.

568 Nebuchadnezzar invades Egypt.

562 Nebuchadnezzar dies and is succeeded by his son Amel-marduk (Evil-merodach), who reigns two years. Jehoiachin is released from prison in Babylon.

556 Nabonidus becomes the last king of Babylon. Dissention occurs in Babylon, and Nabonidus transfers his residence to Tema in the Arabian Desert, remaining there until 545.

550 Cyrus rises in Persia and defeats Astyages and the Medes in battle.

547 Cyrus campaigns against Lydia and conquers most of Ionia.

II Isaiah

539 Cyrus and the Persians take Babylon, marking the beginning of the Persian Empire

538 Cyrus issues an edict permitting Jews to return to their homeland. Sheshbazzar, a son of Jehoiachin, is made governor of Judah and put in charge of returning to the Jews sacred vessels taken by Nebuchadnezzar to Babylon.

III Isaiah

530 Cyrus dies after taking his own life in battle; he is succeeded by his oldest son, Cambyses. More Jews return to Palestine.

525 Cambyses conquers Egypt but spares the Jewish temple in Elephantine; Egypt is now under Persian rule. More small groups of Jews return to Palestine.

Prophets in the Sixth and Fifth Centuries

522 Cambyses dies; Darius I becomes King of Persia.

Haggai

Zechariah

520 Work begins to rebuild the Temple in Jerusalem; Zerubbabel, nephew of Sheshbazzar, is now present in Jerusalem where he has been appointed governor. He is credited with laying the foundations of the Temple. Joshua the high priest is also in Jerusalem directing spiritual affairs.

515 Work on the Temple is finished, and the Temple is dedicated.

486 Darius I dies and is succeeded by his son Xerxes I.

465 Xerxes I is assassinated and succeeded by his son Artaxerxes I, who becomes king of Persia.

A Jewish colony is in existence at Elephantine in Egypt during the entire fifth century. In Greece the the Golden Age of Pericles, Socrates, Sophocles, and others begins, lasting roughly until 424, the year Artaxerxes I dies.

II Zechariah

458 Ezra is granted permission to go to Jerusalem and goes with a large company. After his arrival, he reads the Torah to people in Jerusalem. The Feast of Booths is celebrated.

Malachi

445   Nehemiah, cupbearer to Artaxerxes I, is appointed governor of Judah and given permission to begin rebuilding the walls of Jerusalem. He is subsequently appointed governor of Judah.

440   Nehemiah is now in Jerusalem, where work begins on restoring the fortifications of Jerusalem. Nehemiah remains in Jerusalem until 433, when he returns to the Persian court. He later petitions the king to return to Jerusalem, and is granted a return.

Joel

431   The Peloponnesian War, between Athens and Sparta, begins.

424   King Artaxerxes I, Nehemiah's patron, dies and is succeeded by Xerxes II (423), then by Darius II (423–404).

404   Artaxerxes II becomes king of Persia at the death of Darius II. Persia intervenes in support of Sparta, ending the Peloponnesian War.

REFLECTION

1. Do you believe that Zion (Jerusalem) is still "the apple of the Lord's eye," and that in the end of days it will be where all nations go to learn the ways of God?

2. Jeremiah was opposed to prophets reporting their dreams. Dreams otherwise in the Bible were taken as a source of divine revelation. Can dreams be taken as divine revelation today?

3. Ezekiel was called to be a watchman over his people. Do you ever think of your priest or pastor as being a watchman? Why or why not?

4. The Messianic prophecy in Isa 65:25 says that the wolf and lamb shall feed together, the lion shall eat straw like the ox, and dust shall be the serpent's food. Did any of this happen when the Messiah came?

HAGGAI

3

PEOPLE SAY: "IT IS NOT TIME TO REBUILD YAHWEH'S HOUSE" (1:1-2)

1 ¹In the second year of Darius the king, in the sixth month, on the first day of the month, the word of Yahweh came by the prophet Haggai to Zerubbabel son of Shealtiel, governor of Judah, and to Joshua son of Jehozadak, the high priest: ²Thus said Yahweh of hosts: This people says the time has not yet come to rebuild Yahweh's house.

RHETORIC AND COMPOSITION

THIS BOOK LACKS A superscription like most prophetic books, opening instead with a beginning word from Yahweh to the prophet Haggai. The same obtains in the book of Zechariah. The present verses are delimited in the Hebrew Bible by a section after 1:2.

MESSAGE

Yahweh's word came by Haggai to Zerubbabel in the second year of Darius (i.e., 520), in the sixth month, the month of Elul (Neh 6:15; 1 Macc 14:27), which would be in August or September. All Haggai's prophecies come in three and a half months within this year (Wolff). Haggai receives mention elsewhere, in Ezra 5:1 and 6:14. Zerubbabel was the son of Shealtiel (Gk. Salathiel in the genealogies of Matt 1:12 and Luke 3:27), grandson of young King Jehoiachin, who was taken by Nebuchadnezzar to Babylon in 598 (2 Kgs 24:10–15; 1 Chr 3:16–17). Zerubbabel thus came from the royal, Davidic line, having been appointed governor in the Persian province of Judah. Joshua was the first high priest in the restored community, called Jeshua in Ezra 2:2 and 3:2 and in Neh 12:1. He was the son of Jehozadak (Jozadak), who was taken into exile by the Babylonians in 586 (1 Chr 6:15 [Heb. 5:41]), and the grandson of the high priest Seraiah, who was put to death by Nebuchadnezzar at Riblah after Jerusalem fell (2 Kgs 25:18–21; Jer 52:24–27). We have here the oldest use of the term "high priest" in the OT (Mitchell). Ezra the scribe was also a son of Seraiah (Ezra 7:1).

A small community of returned exiles had been in Jerusalem for eighteen years, but Haggai learned from Yahweh that this people was saying it was not time to rebuild the Temple (cf. Ezek 11:3). Yahweh shows displeasure in the words "this people" (Mitchell). Although Cyrus in the first year of his reign had given orders that the Jerusalem sanctuary be rebuilt (Ezra 6:3), Judahites had been unable to rebuild (Ezra 4:1–5). Samaritans up north offered to help in the rebuilding, saying they could worship along with the Judahites, but Zerubbabel and Joshua rejected the idea out of hand, and subsequent events made Judahites afraid to

People Say: "It Is Not Time to Rebuild Yahweh's House" (1:1–2)

rebuild. Haggai's entire prophecy is set over against this unwillingness to rebuild.

REFLECTION

1. Haggai's prophecies were given during a brief period of three and a half months. Do you think he might have prophesied for a longer time?
2. Why do you think people felt it was not time to rebuild the Temple? See Ezra 4:1–5.
3. The Samaritans up north later decided to build their own temple on Mount Gerizim (cf. John 4:1–42). Who were the Samaritans? See 2 Kgs 17:5–41.

4

YOU HAVE SOWN MUCH, BUT HARVESTED LITTLE (1:3-6)

1 ³Then the word of Yahweh came by Haggai the prophet: ⁴Is it a time for you yourselves to live in your paneled houses while this house lies in ruins? ⁵Now therefore thus said Yahweh of hosts: Take to heart your ways! ⁶You have sown much, but harvested little; you eat, but never have enough; you drink, but never have your fill; you clothe yourselves, but no one is warm; and the one earning wages earns to put it into a bag with holes.

RHETORIC AND COMPOSITION

THESE VERSES ARE DELIMITED by sections in the Hebrew Bible. The *BHS*, the *BHQ*, Wolff, and Petersen scan 1:4-6 and certain others in Haggai as poetry, but the RSV and NRSV, like the original *BHK*, take all verses in the book to be prose. The style of this prophet is question and answer. "Take heart to your ways" in 1:5 is a link phrase to "take heart to your ways" in 1:7.

MESSAGE

Haggai turns the people's words upon themselves: If it is not time to build Yahweh's house, is it time for you to live in paneled houses while Yahweh's house lies in ruins? (1:4; cf. 2 Sam 7:2). Paneling was probably in cedar (Jer 22:14), which adorned the first Temple (1 Kgs 6:9). The paneled houses may have been those of Zerubbabel and Joshua since most of the people were desperately poor (Achtemeier). "Covered houses" may also be taken to mean "roofed houses," as cedar beams were used in the roofing of large rooms (Wolff; cf. 1 Kgs 6:9; 7:3). The prophet says further: Take to heart your ways! Things have not been going well: crops have been poor; people have not enough to eat, are unable to resist the cold, and are impoverished (1:6; cf. 2:15-17). Perhaps a reason exists for all this.

REFLECTION

1. Does it happen today that people take care of their own needs before they attend to the Lord's work? Recall David's word to Samuel in 2 Sam 7:1-3.

2. What do you think "Take heart to your ways" means?

3. Do poor harvests have anything to do with displeasure of the Lord?

5

"GO UP TO THE HILLS, BRING WOOD AND BUILD THE HOUSE" (1:7–11)

1 ⁷Thus said Yahweh of hosts: Take to heart your ways! ⁸Go up to the hills and bring wood and build the house and I will take pleasure in it, and I will be glorified, said Yahweh. ⁹You looked for much, and behold, it came to little; and when you brought it home, I blew it away. Because of what? oracle of Yahweh of hosts. Because of my house that lies in ruins while you hurry off everyone to his own house. ¹⁰Therefore the heavens above you have withheld the dew and the earth has withheld its produce. ¹¹And I have called for a drought upon the land, and upon the hills, and upon the grain, and upon the new wine, and upon the oil, and upon what the soil produces, and upon humans, and upon animals, and upon all their labors.

"Go Up to the Hills, Bring Wood and Build the House" (1:7–11)

RHETORIC AND COMPOSITION

THESE VERSES ARE DELIMITED by sections in the Hebrew Bible. Haggai is giving another oracle from Yahweh. 1:11 has a ninefold repetition of the preposition "upon." "Take heart to your ways" in 1:7 is a link phrase to "take heart to your ways" in 1:5. The *BHS* and *BHQ* scan these verses as poetry.

MESSAGE

The prophet tells the people to take another thing to heart. Yahweh says: Go up into the hills, bring wood, and build Yahweh's house, and I will take pleasure in it and be glorified by worship of my name in the sanctuary. Judah's hills were thickly wooded at the time (Neh 2:8; 8:15–16), and from the forests on Mount Carmel (Amos 9:3) one could always cut trees. Before the new Temple's foundation was laid, Judahites were said to have paid Sidonians and Tyrians to bring cedars from Lebanon (Ezra 3:6–7). Haggai repeats again that people have fared poorly of late, and what they managed to bring home Yahweh blew away. Why? The prophet answers his own question. Because Yahweh's house lay in ruins while everyone was hurrying off to his own house. The heavens above had been bronze and the earth hard as iron (cf. Deut 28:23), and it was Yahweh's doing. The drought called forth by Yahweh will affect grain, wine, and oil, Judah's three principal crops (Deut 7:13; 11:14; 12:17; Jer 31:12), but much more—people, animals, and human labor. But Yahweh says elsewhere that he will reverse all this once the Temple is rebuilt (Zech 8:12).

REFLECTION

1. Do we build churches today that God may be glorified in it?
2. How do we justify church buildings in light of Jesus' words in John 4:21–24?
3. When church buildings have been destroyed by war, fire, or natural disasters, is it not natural to want to rebuild them? The Frauenkirche in Dresden was rebuilt after its destruction by Allied bombs in 1945, and the Notre-Dame Cathedral in Paris is currently being rebuilt after its fire in 2019; however, the Kaiser Wilhelm Kirche in Berlin was left in partial ruins after its destruction in 1943.

6

WORK BEGINS ON YAHWEH'S HOUSE (1:12-15)

1 ¹²Then Zerubbabel son of Shealtiel, and Joshua son of Jehozadak, the high priest, with all the remnant of the people, obeyed the voice of Yahweh their God, and the words of the prophet Haggai, as Yahweh their God had sent him; and the people feared Yahweh. ¹³Then Haggai, the messenger of Yahweh, spoke Yahweh's message to the people, saying, I am with you, oracle of Yahweh. ¹⁴And Yahweh stirred up the spirit of Zerubbabel son of Shealtiel, governor of Judah, and the spirit of Joshua son of Jehozadak, the high priest, and the spirit of all the remnant of the people; and they came and did work in the house of Yahweh of hosts their God, ¹⁵on the twenty-fourth day of the month, in the sixth month.

RHETORIC AND COMPOSITION

The Hebrew Bible delimits 1:12–14 with sections, but the chapter division takes Hebrew 1:15 with what follows, which is the more likely beginning of the following prophecy (cf. 1:1). If 1:15 goes with what precedes (Driver; Petersen), it dates the beginning of work on the Temple; if it goes with chapter 2 (Wolff), it dates the prophecy that follows.

MESSAGE

This brief passage reports that Haggai's word from Yahweh influenced Zerubbabel (governor of the province), Joshua the high priest, and the remnant community to begin the work of rebuilding Yahweh's house (cf. Ezra 5:2). Driver thinks this was only the preliminary work of clearing away the rubble (cf. 2:15–19). Of more importance is that people obeyed and now feared Yahweh. Haggai here is called a "messenger of Yahweh," a designation commonly reserved for the Hebrew prophet (cf. Isa 6:8; Jer 1:7). "I am with you" is God's preeminent promise, repeated in 2:4 and found throughout Scripture (Gen 28:15; Exod 3:12; Josh 1:5; Judg 6:16; Jer 1:8, 19; 15:20; 30:11; Isa 41:10; 43:5; Matt 28:20; cf. Matt 1:23). In Exod 3:14 "I am" becomes the secret divine name (Lundbom 1978).

REFLECTION

1. Haggai, like other OT prophets, is called a "messenger/angel of Yahweh." What comparable term would we use for such a person in society today?

2. Is Yahweh's "I am with you" promise sufficient for you in a time of testing or loss?

Work Begins on Yahweh's House (1:12–15)

3. How often does preaching from one of God's ministers influence the governor today?

7

WHO IS LEFT THAT REMEMBERS YAHWEH'S FORMER HOUSE? (2:1-5)

2 ¹ In the second year of King Darius, in the seventh month, on the twenty-first day of the month, the word of Yahweh came by Haggai the prophet: ²Kindly speak to Zerubbabel son of Shealtiel, governor of Judah, and to Joshua son of Jehozadak, the high priest, and to the remnant of the people: ³Who is left among you that saw this house in its former glory? And how do you see it now? Is it not in your eyes as nothing? ⁴Yet now be strong, O Zerubbabel, oracle of Yahweh, and be strong, O Joshua son of Jehozadak, the high priest, and be strong, all you people of the land, oracle of Yahweh, and work, for I am with you, oracle of Yahweh of hosts, ⁵according

Who Is Left that Remembers Yahweh's Former House? (2:1–5)

> to the promise that I made you when you came
> out of Egypt. And my spirit abides among you;
> do not fear.

RHETORIC AND COMPOSITION

THE BEGINNING OF THIS passage is marked by the chapter division at 2:1, whereas the Hebrew Bible had a section after 1:14. The Hebrew Bible has another section after 2:5. Haggai puts forth three questions to Zerubbabel, Joshua, and the people, and with repetitive rhetoric admonishes the same to be strong and begin the work. The *BHS* and *BHQ* scan 2:3–5 as poetry.

MESSAGE

Haggai here is addressing Zerubbabel, Joshua, and the remnant people with questions they doubtless were harboring in their own minds. Does anyone among them remember Solomon's Temple in its former glory? Only some of the most aged would. Before them lay a pile of rubble, what Nebuchadnezzar and his army left behind after destroying Jerusalem in 586 (2 Kgs 25:8–9; Jer 52:12–13). Haggai asks if they see the rubble as nothing. Of course they do. But the prophet tells all to be strong, to take courage (cf. Ezra 10:4; 1 Chr 28:20), and to get on with the work, for Yahweh is with them, reminding them of promises Yahweh made when they were about to leave Egypt (Exod 3:12; 33:14). The people should also remember prophecies of Ezekiel (Ezek 40–48) and III Isaiah (Isa 60:13; 61:4) about a new and more splendid Temple, which Haggai envisions in his next oracle. Yahweh's spirit abides with his people (Zech 4:6); they need not fear.

REFLECTION

1. The Solomonic Temple was destroyed in 586; it was now 520. How old would one have to be to remember the former Temple in all its glory?

2. Paul echoes 2:4 in telling members of his churches to "Be strong!" (Rom 15:1; 1 Cor 16:13; Eph 6:10; 2 Tim 2:1), but also says, "when I am weak, then I am strong" (2 Cor 12:10; cf. 13:9). How can we be strong in today's world?

3. If Yahweh's Spirit abides in us, can it keep us from debilitating fear?

8

"THE LATTER GLORY OF THIS HOUSE WILL BE GREATER THAN THE FORMER" (2:6-9)

2 ⁶For thus said Yahweh of hosts: Again, in a little while, and I will shake the heavens and the earth and the sea and the dry land; ⁷and I will shake all the nations, and the treasure of all the nations shall come, and I will fill this house with glory, said Yahweh of hosts. ⁸The silver is mine and the gold is mine, oracle of Yahweh of hosts. ⁹The latter glory of this house will be greater than the former, said Yahweh of hosts; and in this place I will give peace, oracle of Yahweh of hosts.

RHETORIC AND COMPOSITION

THESE VERSES ARE DELIMITED in the Hebrew Bible by sections, but the present oracle continues the prior one, leading Driver, Mitchell, and Achtemeier to end the prior unit at 2:9. The *BHS* and *BHQ* scan these verses as poetry.

MESSAGE

In a dramatic act Yahweh says he will shake the heavens and earth, the sea and dry land (2:6; cf. Heb 12:26–27), also the nations so their treasures will come to fill his house with glory (2:7). The glory will result from the treasures, not the divine presence (Driver; Wolff). There is an echo here of the prophecies of II and III Isaiah (Isa 45:14; 60:5, 11, 13, 16; 61:6; cf. Rev 21:24). Wealth of the nations came to Solomon (1 Kgs 9:28; 10:14–22, 27). Silver and gold, however, belong not to the nations but to Yahweh. Haggai says the latter-glory of Yahweh's house will be greater than the former, and residing in this house will be his ultimate blessing: peace (Isa 60:17–18). The Temple was completed four years later (Ezra 6:15).

G. F. Handel's *Messiah* takes one verse from this prophecy:

Part 1

Movement 1: Overture (symphony only)

Movement 5: Hag 2:6–7

> Thus saith the Lord of Hosts; yet once, a little while, and I will shake the heavens, and the earth, the sea, and the dry land; And I will shake all nations; and the Desire of All Nations shall come.

"The Latter Glory of This House Will Be Greater Than the Former" (2:6–9)

REFLECTION

1. What did Handel mean when he spoke of the Lord of hosts shaking the heavens, the earth, the sea, the dry land, and all the nations?
2. Does the Lord fill our churches with his glory? What is that glory?
3. Peace is not simply quiet; it is well-being. Does the Lord give this peace in our churches?

9

BEFORE AND AFTER THE FOUNDATION WAS LAID (2:10–19)

2 ¹⁰In the twenty-fourth day of the ninth month, in the second year of Darius, the word of Yahweh came to Haggai the prophet: ¹¹Thus said Yahweh of hosts: Kindly ask the priests for a ruling: ¹²If one carries consecrated meat in the fold of his garment, and with the fold touches bread, or stew, or wine, or oil, or any food, does it become holy? The priests answered, "No." ¹³Then Haggai said, "Should one who is unclean by contact with a dead body touch any of these, does it become unclean? The priests answered, "It will become unclean." ¹⁴Then Haggai said, So is this people, and so is this nation before me, oracle of Yahweh; and so is every work of their hands; and that which they offer there is unclean.

Before and After the Foundation Was Laid (2:10-19)

¹⁵But now, kindly take to heart from this day and onward, from before a stone was laid upon a stone in Yahweh's Temple, ¹⁶during all that time, when one came to a heap of twenty measures, there were but ten; when one came to the wine vat to draw out fifty measures, there were but twenty. ¹⁷I struck all the work of your hands with blight and mildew and hail, and you came not to me, oracle of Yahweh. ¹⁸Kindly take to heart from this day and onward, from the twenty-fourth day of the ninth month, from the day that the foundation of Yahweh's Temple was laid, take to heart: ¹⁹Is the seed yet in the barn? Do even the vine and the fig tree and the pomegranate and the olive tree yield nothing? From this day I will bless you.

RHETORIC AND COMPOSITION

THESE VERSES ARE DELIMITED by sections in the Hebrew Bible. The passage begins with questions and answers: this time the prophet questions the priests and they answer. More repetitive language characterizes the time before as well as the time after the foundation of Yahweh's new Temple was laid. The *BHS* and *BHQ* scan 2:14–18a as poetry.

MESSAGE

On the twenty-fourth day of the ninth month, roughly three months after work had begun on the Temple (1:14–15), Haggai is told by Yahweh to get a ruling from the priests on two points of ceremonial observance (cf. Lev 10:10–11). If one carries consecrated meat in his garment and his garment touches other kind of food, does that food become holy. They answered "No." Had the consecrated meat touched not the garment but other food, the answer would have been "Yes" (cf. Lev 6:27). A second question: If one has had contact with a dead body and touches any of these, does it become unclean? They answered "Yes" (cf. Num 19:11–22). Haggai then makes a comparison. People and their sacrificial offerings have been rendered unclean before Yahweh. How so? Before one stone was laid upon another in rebuilding the Temple, there was a small yield and privation on every front (cf. Amos 4:9). Haggai pointed this out in his first oracle (1:6). But once the foundation was laid, everything changed. The prophet then asks rhetorically, "Is there seed (yet to be sown) in the barn?" No. And, "Do all the fruit trees bear nothing?" Of course not. Yahweh says that from this day on he will bless the people; accompanying this promise is an unspoken admonition that the people must proceed with all haste to complete the Temple's rebuilding. Between the oracles in 2:1–5 and 2:6–9 and the present oracle is the prophecy recorded in Zech 1:1–6.

REFLECTION

1. Do you recall the day when the cornerstone was laid on your church building? Was it not a day of great celebration?

10

ZERUBBABEL TO BE YAHWEH'S CHOSEN ONE (2:20-23)

2 ²⁰The word of Yahweh came a second time to Haggai on the twenty-fourth day of the month: ²¹Speak to Zerubbabel, governor of Judah: I am about to shake the heavens and the earth, ²²and I will overthrow the throne of kingdoms, and I am about to destroy the strength of the kingdoms of the nations, and I will overthrow the chariots and their riders; and the horses and their riders shall fall, every one by the sword of his brother. ²³On that day, oracle of Yahweh of hosts, I will take you, O Zerubbabel son of Shealtiel, my servant, oracle of Yahweh, and I will make you like a signet ring, for I have chosen you, oracle of Yahweh of hosts.

RHETORIC AND COMPOSITION

This passage is delimited by a section in the Hebrew Bible before 2:20; the final verse ends the book. The *BHS* and *BHQ* scan 2:21b–22 as poetry.

MESSAGE

This passage is addressed to Zerubbabel, governor of Judah, for whom Yahweh has a special word. Haggai is told to speak to Zerubbabel and tell him that Yahweh once more is about to shake the heavens and earth (cf. 2:6), this time to overthrow the nations and inaugurate the Messianic Age. Zerubbabel, like David (1 Kgs 8:16; 11:34), will be Yahweh's chosen one, marked for honor by being given his signet ring (cf. Jer 22:24). In the book of Zechariah Zerubbabel is credited with laying the foundation of the Temple (Zech 4:7–10). The present prophecy, at least as a Messianic prediction, went unfulfilled. Zerubbabel disappeared without a trace.

REFLECTION

1. Zerubbabel was believed in his time to be the Messiah. Others came later who claimed to be "somebody" or were claimed by others to be "somebody" (Acts 5:33–39). How did people know that Jesus was the Messiah?

ZECHARIAH

11

CALL TO REPENTANCE (1:1-6)

1 ¹In the eighth month, in the second year of Darius, the word of Yahweh came to Zechariah son of Berechiah son of Iddo, the prophet: ²Yahweh was very angry with your fathers, ³so you should say to them, Thus said Yahweh of hosts: Return to me, oracle of Yahweh of hosts, and I will return to you, said Yahweh of hosts. ⁴Do not be like your fathers, to whom the former prophets proclaimed: 'Thus said Yahweh of hosts, Return would you from your evil ways and from your evil doings. But they did not listen or heed me, oracle of Yahweh. ⁵Your fathers, where are they? And the prophets, do they live forever? ⁶But my words and my statutes that I commanded my servants the prophets, did they not overtake your fathers? So, they repented and said, As Yahweh of hosts purposed to do to us according to our ways and doings, thus he has done with us.

ZECHARIAH

RHETORIC AND COMPOSITION

THIS OPENING PASSAGE IS delimited at its conclusion by a section in the Hebrew Bible after 1:6. The *BHS* scans 1:3b and 5–6, and the *BHQ* has 1:2–3, 4b–6 as poetry; Petersen also sees poetry here, but the RSV and NRSV take the verses as prose. The Versions credit Zechariah with being a poet (Mitchell: 83), and in the LXX his name appears in titles to Pss 145–48, and in some Greek manuscripts, to Ps 137 (138). Like the book of Haggai, so this book has no superscription, proceeding straightaway to give Zechariah's first oracle, spoken in the second year of Darius, in the eighth month. According to the book that bears his name, Zechariah is the grandson, not son, of Iddo the priest (*contra* Ezra 5:1; 6:14; Neh 12:16).

MESSAGE

Zechariah begins his prophecy by saying that Yahweh is very angry with the people's ancestors, so he is to call them to return (i.e., repent) and not be like the ancestors to whom the former prophets spoke this same message (cf. Hos 14:2–4; Jer 3:12–15; 18:11; 25:4–5; 35:15), but who did not return (Amos 4:6–12; Jer 7:24; 29:19; 35:16–17). These Judahites, having just *returned* from exile, must now *return* to Yahweh. On the expression, "your (evil) ways and (evil) doings," see Jer 7:3, 5; 17:10; 18:11; 23:22; 25:5; 26:3, 13. The prophet then asks, Where are the ancestors now, and where also are the (false) prophets? The obvious answer is that they are dead, having come under the curses promised in Deut 28:15–68. Yahweh's words and statutes, given by Yahweh's servants the prophets, did they not overtake the fathers? Of course they did. Others repented, not at the warning, but when judgment forced them to it. This prophecy was also spoken between Haggai's two oracles in 2:1–5 and 2:6–9.

Call to Repentance (1:1–6)

REFLECTION

1. Does the Lord becomes angry with Christians today?
2. Are there false prophets in our own day? How do we identify them?
3. Repentance is difficult, very difficult. But is it not better to repent when warned than having to do it after judgment has come?

12

YAHWEH IS RETURNING TO JERUSALEM WITH COMPASSION (1:7-17)

1 ⁷On the twenty-fourth day of the eleventh month—it was the month of Shebat,[1] in the second year of Darius, the word of Yahweh came to Zechariah son of Berechiah son of Iddo, the prophet: ⁸"I saw in the night, and behold, a man was riding on a red horse! And he was stationed among the myrtle trees that were in the deep, and behind him were red, sorrel, and white horses. ⁹Then I said, "What are these, my lord?" And the angel who spoke with me said to me: "I will show you what these are." ¹⁰So the man who was stationed among the myrtle trees answered and said: "These are they whom Yahweh sent to go back and forth in the land." ¹¹Then they

---

1. The name of the month in the Babylonian calendar, similarly Chislev in 7:1.

answered the angel who stood among the myrtle trees and said: "We have been going back and forth through the land, and behold, all the land sits still and is quiet." [12]Then the angel of Yahweh answered and said: "O Yahweh of hosts, how long will you not show compassion on Jerusalem and the cities of Judah, against whom you have been angry these seventy years?" [13]Then Yahweh answered the angel who spoke with me with good and comforting words. [14]So the angel who spoke with me said to me, "Proclaim saying: Thus said Yahweh of hosts, I am jealous for Jerusalem and for Zion, very jealous. [15]And I am very angry with the nations that are at ease, for while I was only a little angry, they helped turn it into evil. [16]Therefore thus said Yahweh: I am returning to Jerusalem with compassion; my house shall be rebuilt in it, oracle of Yahweh of hosts, and a measuring line shall be stretched out over Jerusalem. [17]Proclaim again saying: Thus said Yahweh of hosts: My cities shall again overflow with prosperity, and Yahweh will again comfort Zion and again choose Jerusalem."

RHETORIC AND COMPOSITION

THESE VERSES ARE DELIMITED by sections in the Hebrew Bible. The *BHS* and *BHQ* scan 1:14b–17 as poetry, but the RSV and NRSV take all the verses as prose. Petersen, here and elsewhere, formats some discourse as poetry or rhythmic prose. A four-fold repetition of "again" occurs in 1:17.

MESSAGE

Here is the first of eight visions that continue to 6:15. Former prophets also received visions from Yahweh (Amos

7:1–9; 8:1–3; cf. 1:1; Jer 1:11–14). On the twenty-fourth day of the eleventh month, in the month of Shebat (February), three months after Zechariah made his call for repentance (1:1–6), and two months after Haggai's encouraging prophecies (Hag 2:18–23), a vision comes taken to be a word from Yahweh. Zechariah sees in the night a man riding on a reddish-brown horse. The horse is stationed among myrtle trees "in the deep" (cf. Ps 107:24), and behind him are horses of three colors. Zechariah's vision is in color! Driver takes the imagined deep place to be a myrtle-covered glen near Jerusalem; Mitchell likewise (cf. the king's garden in 2 Kgs 25:4). But Petersen: 113 thinks the trees were stationed near the cosmic deep ($m^e\d{s}ulāh$), arguing that in Zechariah's vision "we are conveyed to a geography which is not really of this world and is not directly that of the divine dwelling." It is "between worlds." Behind the man are other men on reddish-brown, sorrel (chestnut), and white horses. Who are these? the prophet asks. Perhaps a reflection of Persian patrols, but more likely other "angelic beings, scouts of God, who have come in from patrolling the earth bringing their reports with them" (Driver: 184). "Going back and forth" means patrolling (cf. Job 1:7; 2:2). We have here and in subsequent verses (1:21; 2:3; 3:1; 4:1; 5:2, 5; 6:4) an angel/messenger standing between Yahweh and the prophet. Usually the prophet gets a direct word from Yahweh and is himself the messenger (cf. Hag 1:13). The prophet addresses the angel with the question, "What are these?" The angel says he will show him. The rider on the front horse interposes and explains that the horsemen are scouts Yahweh has sent out to patrol the land. Then the horsemen, speaking for themselves, report that all the land is quiet (cf. Hag 2:6–7, 20–22).

The angel of Yahweh then addresses Yahweh with the question, "How long will you not show compassion in Jerusalem and the cities of Judah, against whom you have been

Yahweh Is Returning to Jerusalem with Compassion (1:7–17)

angry these seventy years?" The stereotyped seventy-year period, mentioned also in 7:5, is the tenure of Babylonian power in the ANE, not the length of Judah's exile or its period of desolation (Jer 25:11; 29:10; *contra* 2 Chr 36:21; Petersen; Meyers; Lundbom 2004: 249). Then Yahweh answers the angel who spoke with the prophet with good and comforting words (cf. Isa 40:1). The angel said the prophet should proclaim to the people that Yahweh is very jealous for Jerusalem (8:2; cf. Exod 20:5; Deut 4:24; 5:9; 34:14; Nah 1:2). He was only a little angry with his covenant people (although in 1:2 Yahweh is said to be *very* angry). Yahweh now says he is very angry with nations who are at ease, for earlier they just made things worse. Reference here is probably to the Babylonians (Mitchell; Petersen; cf. Isa 47:5–7). Yahweh says he is returning to Jerusalem with compassion, and his house shall be rebuilt in it. A measuring line shall be stretched out over the city (cf. Jer 31:38–40). The prophet is to proclaim that Yahweh's cities shall again overflow with prosperity, and he will comfort Zion and again choose Jerusalem as his city (cf. 1 Kgs 8:44, 48; 2 Chr 6:6, 34, 38).

REFLECTION

1. The great prophet Isaiah "waits for the Lord" (Isa 8:17) and calls on others to do the same (Isa 26:8; 30:18; 33:12); so, too, Habakkuk (Hab 2:3) and Zephaniah (Zeph 3:8). But is not 70 years a long time to wait? Israel had to wait even longer for its Messiah to come, and when he did come, he was received joyfully in the Temple by two people awaiting him (Luke 2:25–38).

2. The prophet says the Lord was very jealous for his people. What does jealous mean here?

13

THE FOUR HORNS AND FOUR IRONSMITHS (1:18-21 [HEB. 2:1-4])

1 ¹⁸And I lifted up my eyes, and I saw, and behold, four horns! ¹⁹And I said to the angel who spoke with me, "What are these?" And he answered me, "These are the horns that have scattered Judah, Israel, and Jerusalem." ²⁰Then Yahweh showed me four smiths. ²¹And I said, "What are they coming to do?" And he answered, "These are the horns that scattered Judah, so that no man could lift up his head; and these have come to terrify them, to strike down the horns of the nations that lifted up their horn against the land of Judah to scatter it."

The Four Horns and Four Ironsmiths (1:18–21 [Heb. 2:1–4])

RHETORIC AND COMPOSITION

THESE VERSES ARE DELIMITED by sections in the Hebrew Bible. In the Hebrew Bible the verses are 2:1–4.

MESSAGE

In this second vision, which follows and fulfills the first, the prophet sees four horns and four ironsmiths. Horns (of oxen) symbolize might (Deut 33:17; Ps 22:12 [Heb. 22:13]), often the might of nations (1 Kgs 22:11; Mic 4:13; Jer 48:25). The prophet speaks to the angel who had been talking with him, and asks, "Who are these?" The angel says they are the powers that destroyed Israel, Judah, and Jerusalem. The number four represents totality, sometimes meaning "from every direction" (cf. "four winds/spirits of heaven" in 2:6 and 6:4–6). Yahweh then shows the prophet four ironsmiths. The horns are made of iron (cf. 1 Kgs 22:11; Mic 4:13). The prophet says, "What are they coming to do?" The angel says the smiths have come to terrify and strike down the nations that scattered (Israel and) Judah so no one could lift up his head. Reference would be to the Assyrians and Babylonians. When one is subjugated, even imprisoned, one cannot lift up one's head (Gen 40:20; Judg 8:28; Jer 52:31).

REFLECTION

1. What must it feel like for a nation that cannot lift up its head?
2. Have you ever felt as if you could not lift up your head? What made you feel this way?

14

A MEASURING LINE FOR JERUSALEM NOT NEEDED (2:1-5 [HEB. 2:5-9])

2 ¹AND I LIFTED up my eyes, and I saw, and behold, a man and in his hand a measuring line! ²Then I said, "Where are you going?" And he said to me, "To measure Jerusalem, to see what is its width and what is its length." ³And behold, the angel who spoke with me came forward, and another angel came forward to meet him ⁴and said to him, "Run, say to this young man: 'Jerusalem shall be inhabited as open regions because of the multitude of people and cattle in her. ⁵For I will be to her, oracle of Yahweh, a wall of fire round about, and I will be the glory in her.'"

RHETORIC AND COMPOSITION

These verses are delimited by sections in the Hebrew Bible. The *BHS* and *BHQ* take Heb. 2:8b–9 as poetry whereas

A Measuring Line for Jerusalem Not Needed (2:1–5 [Heb. 2:5–9])

Petersen has all the verses as poetry; the RSV and NRSV take all the verses as prose.

MESSAGE

The prophet in this third vision sees a man with a measuring line in hand. He is on his way to measure the site for a restored city of Jerusalem. The man envisions a city with walls! Then an angel other than the one Zechariah had been talking with came and interrupted the first angel, saying: "Run, say to this young man: 'Jerusalem shall be inhabited as open regions because of the multitude of people and cattle in her" (cf. Isa 49:19–20; 54:2–3). In 1:16, however, Yahweh called for a measuring line to be stretched out over Jerusalem! Here Yahweh will be a wall of fire around the city and will be the glory within her (cf. Ezek 43:1–2, 4–5; Isa 60:1–2, 19; Rev 21:23).

REFLECTION

1. Is not this prediction prophetic hyperbole? Nehemiah came later to build up the walls of Jerusalem, and the Old City has had walls ever since. Old cities in China also had walls.
2. What might it mean that the Lord's glory will reside in Jerusalem?

15

HO, HO ZION! ESCAPE BABYLON (2:6-13 [HEB. 2:10-17])

2 ⁶"Ho! Ho! And flee from the land of the north, oracle of Yahweh; for like the four winds of the heaven I have scattered you abroad, oracle of Yahweh. ⁷Ho Zion! Escape, you who dwell with the daughter of Babylon. ⁸For thus said Yahweh of hosts after Glory sent me to the nations that plundered you: Indeed, he who touches you touches the apple of his eye. ⁹For behold, I am waving my hand over them, and they will become spoil for those who served them (cf. Ezek 39:10b). Then you will know that Yahweh of hosts has sent me.

¹⁰Sing and rejoice, O daughter Zion, for behold, I am coming and will dwell in the midst of you, oracle of Yahweh. ¹¹And many nations will join themselves to Yahweh in that day, and they will

be my people. And I will dwell in the midst of you, and you will know that Yahweh of hosts has sent me to you. ¹²And Yahweh will inherit Judah as his portion in the holy land, and he will again choose Jerusalem. ¹³Be silent, all flesh, before Yahweh, for he has roused himself from his holy habitation.

RHETORIC AND COMPOSITION

THESE VERSES ARE DELIMITED by sections in the Hebrew Bible. Other sections occur after 2:9, 11, and 13. The *BHS*, *BHQ*, and Petersen take Heb. 2:8b–14 as poetry; the RSV and NRSV take the verses as prose. This passage is taken as a lyric epilogue to the third vision.

MESSAGE

With an opening "Ho! Ho!" this oracle invites exiles from countries as far distant as the four winds of heaven (6:5; Jer 39:36), where Yahweh has scattered them, to flee these countries (cf. Jer 50:8; 51:6; Isa 48:20). The twofold *hôy* opening the oracle, occurring also in 2:7, is not the usual invective, "Woe" (Amos 6:1; Isa 5:8, 11, 18, 20, 21–22; 45:9; Jer 22:13), but a call to attention (Isa 55:1) or a forceful invitation: "Ho." The "north" in the OT is generally understood as the place where "powers of disaster are bred" (Berridge 1970: 70; cf. Jer 1:14; 3:18; 6:22; 10:22; 23:8; 50:9; Isa 41:25; Ezek 38:15; 39:2). People of Zion (Isa 52:16b) remaining in distant Babylon are told to escape the place (Jer 50:8; 51:6, 45; Isa 48:20), for Yahweh's judgment is coming upon the nations. The expression "after glory" is difficult. "Glory" (without the article) must refer to Yahweh himself (Mitchell; Meyers; 2:5; cf. Isa 6:3; Ezek 3:23), the sentence perhaps meaning that after the glory vision (2:5) Yahweh has sent Zechariah to announce to the exiles that Glory will attend to nations that plundered them, for anyone touching the covenant people, the tenderest and dearest, touches the apple of Yahweh's eye. For the expression "apple of one's eye," see Deut 32:10; Ps 17:8. The apple (lit. "little man") of the eye is the pupil, referring to the eye's dark center in which one may observe the reflection of others (Rashi; cf. Lundbom 2013: 880). Yahweh is going to wave his hand over the nations so they become plunder for those who served them, especially Judahites. "Waving the hand/fist" is a defiant gesture on the part of Yahweh (Isa 10:32; 11:15; 19:16). People will then know that Yahweh has sent Zechariah as his prophet (4:9; 6:15)—that is, when the prophecy has been fulfilled. In the book of Ezekiel the expression that occurs fifty-four times is, "that you/they will know that I am Yahweh" (Ezek 6:7, 10, 13, 14; and so forth).

Daughter Zion in a second oracle is told to sing and rejoice (Zeph 3:14–15), for Yahweh is coming to dwell in her midst. The prophet then echoes a theme heard often in II-III Isaiah, viz., that in future days many nations will join Israel in the worship of Yahweh, not just anywhere, but in the Jerusalem Temple currently being rebuilt (8:22; cf. Isa 45:14; 55:5; 56:3–7; 60:3; Mic 4:1–2). There they shall be Yahweh's people—a remarkable statement since being Yahweh's people is otherwise a covenant statement reserved for Israel (Exod 6:7; Deut 29:12–13 [Heb. 29:11–12]; Lev 26:12; Jer 30:22; 31:1; etc.). A portent to "God-fearers" of the NT (Acts 10:22; 18:7). Petersen: 181 says:

> And now in the early postexilic period it becomes possible to think of "foreigners" having this same relationship with Yahweh. It is not popular to speak of universalism in the Hebrew Bible, and yet both the text in Isa. 56 just cited

and the short verse we are considering clearly suggest that the Israelite/non-Israelite distinction is losing ground to a distinction between those who venerate Yahweh and those who do not.

Fulfillment of the prophecy that Yahweh will dwell amid his people will be another indication that Yahweh has sent Zechariah as his prophet. Yahweh will again inherit Judah as his portion in the holy land and will again choose Jerusalem (1:17). Let all be in silent awe before Yahweh (cf. Zeph 1:7; Hab 2:20); indeed, Yahweh is ready to move from his holy habitation, which could be heaven (Deut 26:15; 2 Chr 30:27; Jer 25:30), otherwise his earthly Temple (Ps 26:8), since Zechariah has just said that Yahweh will again choose Jerusalem (Petersen). In Hab 2:20 the Jerusalem Temple is intended.

REFLECTION

1. Have you ever used the expression "apple of one's eye"? To whom did it refer?

2. Is not the raised fist today a defiant gesture? Do you think the Lord can do it, even as a gesture to foreign nations?

3. How do we know today that the Lord has sent someone to be his prophet?

4. Do you realize that the prophecy about Gentiles joining Jewish people in the worship of their God is rooted in the OT, that it did not begin with Jesus (John 4:7–26), Paul (Acts 18:6), Philip (Acts 8:4–8, 26–38), Peter (Acts 10), or anyone in the Christian church?

16

I WILL BRING MY SERVANT, THE SHOOT (3:1-10)

3 ¹And he showed me Joshua the high priest standing before the angel of Yahweh, also the Satan standing at his right hand to accuse him. ²Then Yahweh said to the Satan, "Yahweh rebuke you, O Satan! Yes, Yahweh who has chosen Jerusalem rebuke you! Is not this a brand plucked out of the fire?" ³Now Joshua was clothed in filthy garments and stood before the angel. ⁴And he answered and said to those standing before him: "Remove the filthy garments from off him." And to him he said, "See, I have caused your iniquity to be taken from you, and I will clothe you in stately robes." ⁵And I said, "Let them place a clean turban on his head." So, they placed a clean turban on his head and clothed him with garments, the angel of Yahweh standing by. ⁶And the angel of Yahweh directed Joshua: ⁷"Thus said Yahweh of hosts: If you walk in my ways and keep my charge, then

I Will Bring My Servant, the Shoot (3:1–10)

you shall rule my house and shall have charge of my courts, and I will give you the right of access among those who are standing here.
⁸Hear now, O Joshua the high priest, you and your fellows who sit before you, indeed these are men of omen, for behold, I am bringing forth my servant, the Shoot. ⁹For behold, the stone that I have set before Joshua, upon a single stone, are seven eyes, Behold, I will engrave its engraving, oracle of Yahweh of hosts, and I will remove the iniquity of that land in a single day. ¹⁰In that day, oracle of Yahweh of hosts, everyone will invite his fellow under his vine and under his fig tree.

RHETORIC AND COMPOSITION

THIS PASSAGE IS DELIMITED at the top by a section in the Hebrew Bible, and at the bottom by the chapter division. The *BHS* and *BHQ* scan 3:7–10, and Petersen, 3:2–10 as poetry; the RSV and NRSV take all the verses as prose.

MESSAGE

Yahweh in this fourth vision shows Joshua, the high priest, standing before his angel and the Satan. The Satan is at the angel's right ready to accuse the high priest. Joshua is standing trial in a (heavenly) court of law. The Satan appears in the Prologue to Job where he accuses Job of wrongdoing (Job 1:6–12; 2:1–8b). The term Satan (without the article) does not appear as a proper name until 1 Chr 21:1, where he is the one who tempts David. It is Satan the tempter who comes to Jesus and others in the NT (Matt 4:1–11; 16:23; Mark 1:12–13; 8:33; Luke 4:1–13).

Here Yahweh through the angel rebukes the Satan, issuing a second rebuke from the One who has chosen

Jerusalem (1:17; 2:12 [Heb. 2:16]; cf. 1 Kgs 8:44; 11:13). The angel asks the Satan, Is not Joshua (and all Judah) a brand plucked from the fire (cf. Amos 4:11)? Was not Joshua himself a brand plucked out of the fire? His grandfather Seraiah was killed by Nebuchadnezzar at Riblah (2 Kgs 25:18–21; Jer 52:24–27), with he and his father, Jehozadak, were among the survivors in exile. The Satan, in any case, is silenced. As Luther said, "One little word will fell him."[1]

We learn that Joshua is standing before the angel, clothed in filthy garments, which symbolize the prior sin of the Judahites. Filth is an indication of sin (Isa 4:4; Prov 30:12; cf. Rev 3:4). The angel then addresses other members of the heavenly court standing before him: "Remove the filthy garments from off him." Turning to address Joshua, the angel then says: "See, I have caused your iniquity to be taken from you, and I will clothe you in stately robes" (cf. white robes, bright and pure, in Rev 3:4–5; 7:14; 19:8). Zechariah calls for someone to put a clean turban on Joshua's head (cf. Job 29:14). Cardinals, bishops, and other high-ranking clergy in the Roman Catholic, Orthodox, Anglican and Lutheran Churches wear miters on their heads for important ceremonies. For Joshua the investiture is done; the priest is clothed in new garments, and a clean turban is placed on his head. Yahweh's angel stands by. The angel then solemnly instructs Joshua: If you walk in Yahweh's ways and keep his charge (cf. Ezek 44:15; 48:11), you will henceforth have authority in the Temple, including in the courtyards, and give right of entry for those standing by (i.e., the attendant angels [3:4]).

The high priest is further told that fellow Zadokite priests sitting before him, who are men of (good) omen, will together with Joshua see Yahweh bring forth his servant, the Shoot (Jer 23:5; 33:15; KJV "Branch"). "Shoot" is a Messianic

---

1. From "A Mighty Fortress Is Our God."

I Will Bring My Servant, the Shoot (3:1–10)

title, referring here in all probability to Zerubbabel (Hag 2:23; Zech 4:9). In 6:12 the "Shoot" will be Joshua. Isaiah and his sons, with the names given to them, were omens/signs of a brighter future for Israel (Isa 8:18; cf. 8:3–4). Here "the restored priesthood is a pledge of the approach of the Messianic kingdom" (Driver: 197). The stone set before Joshua, a top stone for the Temple rebuilding (Meyers), will have Yahweh's eyes upon it, and upon it Yahweh will engrave an inscription saying that he will remove the iniquity of the land in a single day. Yahweh's eyes indicate a divine presence and divine attention (Pss 11:4; 34:15 [Heb. 34:16] 66:7; Deut 11:12), equated with the seven lights of the lampstand in 4:10b. Mitchell and Petersen, however, think the engraved stone will be an ornament on the priest's (head)dress (cf. Exod 28:9–21, 36–38). The day, in any case, will be a happy one, for everyone will invite his friend to sit under his vine and under his fig tree, an expression symbolizing peace and security (1 Kgs 4:25 [Heb. 5:5]; Mic 4:4; 1 Macc 14:12).

REFLECTION

1. Do you know that (the) Satan, who appears more in the NT than in the Old, is without independent power and is always under the Lord's control? Do you agree with Luther that "one little word will fell him"?

2. Do you ever feel as if you were a brand plucked out of the fire? In what way?

3. Joshua the high priest exchanged filthy clothes, symbolizing his and the nation's sinfulness, for a stately robe. Why do you think (young) people today intentionally wear dirty and tattered clothes? What did garments Elijah wore signify (2 Kgs 1:8), or those of John the Baptist (Matt 3:4)?

17

ZERUBBABEL WILL BRING FORTH THE TOP STONE AMID SHOUTS (4:1–14)

4 ¹And the angel who spoke with me came again and wakened me as a man who is wakened from his sleep. ²And he said to me, "What do you see?" And I said,¹ "I see, and behold, a lampstand all of gold with its bowl on its top, and seven lamps upon it, seven and seven pipes to the lamps upon its top, ³and two olive trees upon it, one on the right of the bowl and one on its left." ⁴And I answered and said to the angel who spoke with me, "What are these, my lord?" ⁵And the angel who spoke with me answered and said to me, "Do you not know what these are?" And I said, "No, my lord." ⁶Then he answered and said to me, "This is the word of Yahweh to

1. Reading "And I said" with the Qere, LXX, and other Versions; Kt has "and he said."

Zerubbabel Will Bring Forth the Top Stone Amid Shouts (4:1–14)

Zerubbabel: Not by might, and not by power, but with my Spirit, said Yahweh of hosts. ⁷What are you, O great mountain? Before Zerubbabel you will become a plain; and he will bring forth the top stone amidst shouts: 'Grace, grace to it!'" ⁸And the word of Yahweh came to me: ⁹"The hands of Zerubbabel have laid the foundation of this house and his hands will complete it. Then you will know that Yahweh of hosts has sent me to you. ¹⁰For whoever has despised the day of small things will rejoice when they see the plummet in the hand of Zerubbabel. These seven are the eyes of Yahweh; they rove about in the whole earth." ¹¹Then I answered and said to him, "What are these two olive trees upon the right and upon the left of the lampstand?" ¹²And a second time I answered and said to him, "What are these two branches of the olive trees that are beside the two golden pipes from which the golden oil² is poured out?" ¹³And he said to me, "Do you not know what these are?" I said, "No, my lord." ¹⁴Then he said, "These are two sons of oil who stand by the Lord of the whole earth."

RHETORIC AND COMPOSITION

THIS PASSAGE IS DELIMITED by chapter divisions at top and bottom. The Hebrew Bible has a section after 4:7, presumably because 4:8 begins another word from Yahweh to the prophet. The *BHS* and *BHQ* scan 4:6–10, and Petersen all of 4:2–14, as poetry; the RSV and NRSV take all the verses as prose. Mitchell, Petersen, and Meyers take 4:6b–10a as a later interpolation.

---

2. Hebrew lacks "oil."

MESSAGE

The prophet here must be wakened from his sleep by the angel who spoke to him previously. In this fifth vision the angel asks Zechariah what he sees. He says, I see a golden lampstand (*menôrat zâhâb*) with a receptacle for oil on its top, and the stand has seven lamps on it and seven pipes on top to supply the lamps with oil. In Solomon's Temple were ten separate golden candlesticks (1 Kgs 7:49; cf. Jer 52:19). Zechariah's lamp, in light of Late Bronze and Iron I archaeological finds, may have been shaped differently from the lampstand in Exod 25:31–40, Solomon's, and later lampstands (Petersen: 220, 222 with drawings; Meyers: 290–91 with drawings). The prophet says he also sees two olive trees on top of the seven-branched candlestick, one on the right and one on the left. Zechariah asks the angel, "What are these, my lord?" The angel says, "Do you not know what these are?" Zechariah says "No." The angel answers with a word from Yahweh to Zerubbabel: Not by human might or power will Zerubbabel accomplish his work on the Temple, but by Yahweh's Spirit that will strengthen him (cf. Hag 2:5). Turning to address a great mountain (apostrophe), the angel says that before Zerubbabel it will become a plain, for Zerubbabel will complete the rebuilding, bringing forth the top stone with shouts of the multitude: "Grace, grace, to it!" or "Beautiful, beautiful to it!" (Freedman and Lundbom, *ḥānan* in *TDOT* 5:26–28, 36).

The prophet receives a further word reiterating what has just been said, viz., that as Zerubbabel has begun the rebuilding of the Temple by laying its foundation, his hands shall also complete it. Zechariah says again that when this prophecy is fulfilled, people will know that Yahweh had sent him (cf. 2:9, 11b; 6:15). "Whoever has despised the day of small things" (Hag 2:3) "will rejoice when they see the plummet in the hand of Zerubbabel," i.e., when they see

Zerubbabel Will Bring Forth the Top Stone Amid Shouts (4:1–14)

the walls of the Temple "rising from day to day under his direction" (Mitchell: 199). Yahweh's seven eyes rove about in the entire earth (cf. 3:9), watching the Temple's progress to completion (Driver; cf. 2 Chr 16:9). But Mitchell and Petersen think the seven eyes are the seven lamps on the lampstand.

Zechariah then asks the angel about the two olive trees upon the right and left of the lampstand. What are they? And a second time he asks about the two branches of the trees that are beside the golden pipes from which oil is poured out. The angel says, "Do you not know what these are?" The prophet answers "No." The angel says, "These are two sons of oil who stand by the Lord of the whole earth." "Sons of oil" denotes anointed individuals, who would be Joshua the high priest and Zerubbabel the governor (cf. 6:9–15).

REFLECTION

1. Do you believe work done under the Lord's spirit is greater than human might or power?

2. Have you ever despised the day of small things only to rejoice about them later?

3. Is not finishing a project more important than beginning it? See Eccl 7:8 and Luke 14:28–30.

18

THE FLYING SCROLL (5:1-4)

5 ¹And again I lifted up my eyes, and I saw, and behold, a flying scroll! ²And he said to me, "What do you see?" And I said, "I see a flying scroll; its length is twenty cubits and its breadth ten cubits." ³Then he said to me, "This is the curse that goes out over the face of the whole land; for everyone who steals will be purged out on the one side according to it, and everyone who swears (falsely) will be purged out on the other side according to it. ⁴I will send it forth, oracle of Yahweh of hosts, and it will enter the house of the thief and the house of him who swears falsely by my name, and it will abide in the midst of his house and will consume its timber and its stones.

The Flying Scroll (5:1–4)

RHETORIC AND COMPOSITION

THE PRESENT PASSAGE HAS no sections of delimitation in the Hebrew Bible. The chapter division marks its upper end.

MESSAGE

In this sixth vision the prophet sees a large scroll of skin or parchment in flight. It is roughly thirty feet long and fifteen feet wide, which means it must be unrolled. The interpreting angel tells Zechariah that inscribed on it is a curse for everyone who steals and commits perjury (5:3), both forbidden in the Decalogue (Exod 20:15–16; Deut 5:19–20). They shall be purged out of the community, not having been acquitted (*pace* Meyers). The curse goes out over the entire land. Driver assumes that because of the colossal size of the scroll many curses must have been written on it. Yahweh says he will send the curse into the house of the thief and the house of him who swears falsely, and it will remain there to consume the house timber and stones (5:4). Destruction of one's house was an ancient form of punishment (Hab 3:13b; Dan 2:5; 3:29; Ezra 6:11).

REFLECTION

1. Why is perjury, forbidden in the Ten Commandments (Exod 20:16; Deut 5:20), such a serious crime? What controls do we have over perjury in today's courts?

2. Another of the Ten Commandments is "Do not steal" (Exod 20:15; Deut 5:19). But are not the poor sometimes allowed to get away with stealing from the rich? What about Robin Hood?

19

WICKEDNESS IN A BASKET (5:5-11)

5 ⁵Then the angel who spoke with me came forth and said to me, "Lift up now your eyes and see what is this going forth." ⁶And I said, "What is it?" And he said, "This is the ephah that goes forth." And he said, "This is their eye in all the land." ⁷And behold, a round cover of lead was lifted, and there was one woman sitting in the ephah! ⁸And he said, "This is Wickedness." And he cast her back down into the ephah and cast down a lead stone upon its mouth. ⁹Then I lifted up my eyes and I saw, and behold, two women coming forward with wind in their wings! And their wings were like the wings of a stork. And they lifted up the ephah between earth and heaven. ¹⁰Then I said to the angel who spoke with me, "Where are they taking the ephah?" ¹¹And he said to me, "To build for it a house in

Wickedness in a Basket (5:5–11)

the land of Shinar; and it will be established and
rest there upon its base."

RHETORIC AND COMPOSITION

THE PRESENT PASSAGE IS delimited at top by the chapter division and at bottom by a section in the Hebrew Bible. The Hebrew Bible has another section concluding 5:8.

MESSAGE

Zechariah in this seventh vision is told by the angel who had been speaking to him to lift up his eyes and see what was going forth (5:5). He does, and asks, "What is it?" (5:6). The angel says it is an ephah going forth. An ephah is a unit of dry measure for grain, flour, and the like, equivalent to more or less a bushel. The angel then says, "This is their eye in all the land" (5:6). "Eye" can mean "resemblance" or "appearance" (Num 11:7), but the LXX, reading a slightly different Hebrew word, translates "wrongdoing" (ἀδικία), which points ahead to the wickedness contained in the basket. In either case the basket or wickedness is said to exist throughout the land.

Then behold, a round cover of lead over the basket is lifted, and a woman is sitting there (5:7). She is either an unusually small woman or the basket is unusually large! The scroll of the previous vision was also larger than life (5:2). The angel then says, "This is Wickedness" (5:8) where "Wickedness" (with the article) likely represents idolatry (Mitchell; Meyers). The angel casts the woman down into the basket and with the same intensity casts down a lead stone upon its opening (5:8). Was the woman trying to escape?

The prophet again lifts up his eyes and sees two women coming forward. They have outspread wings and are apparently in flight, lifting the basket to a height between heaven and earth. The women have wings like a stork (5:9). Migrating storks overflying Palestine (Jer 8:7) have strong wings, fly at great heights, and can fly great distances. H. B. Tristram says of the bird:

> During the whole of April [the stork] covers the land, suddenly appearing in the south and moving northwards a few miles a day. Thus we heard at Gennesaret that the country about Samaria was covered with storks, when we had not seen one. Two days afterwards they overspread our neighborhood; not close together, but scattered over hill and valley, plain and marsh alike, steadily quartering the ground about 100 yards apart, picking up snakes, lizards, frogs, or fish, according to the locality... (Tristram 1884: 111; cf. 1898: 246–47).

Zechariah then asks the angel where these women are taking the basket. He says, to build for it a house in the land of Shinar (i.e., Babylonia; cf. Gen 11:2; Isa 11:11), the home of all that is evil, and it will be established and rest permanently there on its base (5:11). The "house" is doubtless a temple (Mitchell; Meyers), a ziggurat as portrayed in Gen 11:4. Exiles having returned from Babylon, wicked idolatry will now return to Babylon where it belongs.

REFLECTION

1. Have you thought of the "tower" in the Gen 11:4 story as a religious temple? In that story God rejects a Babylonian temple and instead chooses Abraham living in Babylon, promising to make of him a great nation (Gen 12:1–3).

20

THE FOUR CHARIOTS (6:1-8)

6 ¹And again I lifted up my eyes, and I saw, and behold, four chariots were going forth from between two mountains, and the mountains were mountains of bronze. ²With the first chariot were red horses, and with the second chariot black horses, ³and with the third chariot white horses, and with the fourth chariot strong spotted horses. ⁴Then I answered and said to the angel who spoke with me, "What are these, my lord?" ⁵And the angel answered and said to me, "These are the four winds of heaven going forth from standing before the Lord of all the earth. ⁶The black horses go forth toward the north country, and the white ones go forth after them, and the spotted ones go forth toward the south country." ⁷Then the strong (spotted) ones that went forth were impatient to go about in the earth. ⁸Then he cried and said to me, "See, those going forth toward the north country have set my spirit at rest in the north country."

RHETORIC AND COMPOSITION

THE PRESENT PASSAGE IS delimited in the Hebrew Bible by sections at beginning and end. Petersen scans the verses as poetry; the *BHS, BHQ*, RSV, and NRSV take the verses as prose. This last vision appears to balance the first (1:7–17). Both feature horses of color, and in both, horses (and riders) are sent to patrol the earth. Both also express Yahweh's anger—in 1:15 with other nations, and in 6:8 only with Babylon (inclusio).

MESSAGE

In this eighth vision the prophet sees four chariots pulled by horses of different colors going forth from between two mountains of bronze. Chariots and horses signify warfare (cf. 9:10). Zechariah wants to know what these chariots and horses represent. The angel says they are the four winds of heaven (cf. 2:6 [Heb. 2:10]; Jer 49:36; Ezek 37:9) going forth from being stationed before the Lord of all the earth. The four winds going forth, doubtless from between the two heavenly mountains, are messengers of Yahweh (cf. Ps 104:4). The black horses are headed for the north country, i.e., Babylonia (2:6–7); the white horses are going after them (Petersen following A. B. Ehrlich emends the Hebrew to read "to the west"; cf. the RSV and NRSV), and the spotted ones are headed toward the south country. We don't know where the reddish-brown horses (cf. 1:8) are headed. The strong steeds, who are the spotted horses, are impatient to get on with patrolling the earth (6:7; cf. 1:10–11). But Yahweh's concern is only with the horses headed to the north country: Yahweh cries out to Zechariah that with them his spirit (here "his anger"; 6:8; cf. Judg 8:3; Eccl 10:4) is set at rest, i.e., is quieted (cf. Ezek 5:13), by being poured forth upon Babylon.

The Four Chariots (6:1-8)

REFLECTION

1. Here is another word of judgment against Babylon. Do you think this would encourage more Jews to leave Babylon and return to Judah?

21

JOSHUA ALSO CROWNED THE SHOOT (6:9-15)

6 ⁹And the word of Yahweh came to me: ¹⁰"Take from the company of exiles, from Heldai, and from Tobijah, and from Jedaiah, who have come from Babylon, and come the same day and go into the house of Josiah son of Zephaniah, ¹¹and take silver and gold and make crowns and set (one) upon the head of Joshua son of Jehozadak, the high priest, ¹²and say to him, 'Thus said Yahweh of hosts: Behold, a man, his name is "Shoot." Yes, from out of his place he will shoot up and build the Temple of Yahweh. ¹³Yes, he will build the Temple of Yahweh and will bear majesty and sit and rule upon his throne, and he will be a priest upon his throne, and peaceful counsel will be between the two of them." ¹⁴And the crowns will be to Helem[1] and to Tobijah and to Jedaiah

1. In 6:10 this individual is called Heldai; Petersen suggests Helem may be a nickname used among friends.

Joshua Also Crowned the Shoot (6:9–15)

and to Hen[2] son of Zephaniah for a memorial in the Temple of Yahweh. ¹⁵And those who are far off will come and build in the Temple of Yahweh; then you will know that Yahweh of hosts has sent me to you. And this will happen if you diligently obey the voice of Yahweh your God.

RHETORIC AND COMPOSITION

THE PRESENT PASSAGE IS delimited at top and bottom by sections in the Hebrew Bible.

BHS and *BHQ* scan 6:12b–13 and Petersen, 6:9–15 as poetry; the RSV and NRSV take all the verses as prose. The passage is a symbolic act by the prophet (Mitchell; Achtemeier).

MESSAGE

Zechariah here receives a word from Yahweh (6:9). He is to take from the company of exiles Heldai, Tobijah, and Jedaiah, who have come from Babylon, and go the same day to the house of Josiah (6:10), who is perhaps a metalworker. The prophet is then to take silver and gold, which the returnees have brought with them from Babylon, and make crowns, setting one on the head of Joshua the high priest (6:10). It is a symbolic act, with the three men acting as witnesses. Zechariah is then to speak this word from Yahweh: "Behold, a man, his name is "Shoot." Yes, from out of his place he will shoot up and build the Temple of Yahweh." In 3:8 Zerubbabel was the Shoot and in Hag 2:23 was to be Yahweh's "signet ring," both Messianic designations (cf. Jer 22:24; 23:5; 33:15). Zerubbabel was the key person in the

---

2. In 6:10 this individual is called Josiah; Petersen suggests Hen, too, may be a nickname used among friends.

Temple rebuilding (4:1–10), but here, as in 4:14, Zechariah anticipates two "anointed ones," which explains the use of "crowns" (plural) in 6:11 and 14. The respective prophecies for both Zerubbabel and Joshua are Messianic. It is noteworthy that in the Qumran *Manual of Discipline* (ix 8–11, 63) the Essenes expect both a priestly and a lay Messiah (Gaster 1976: 6, 63).

Joshua shall bear royal majesty, sitting and bearing rule on his throne with peaceful counsel existing between the two leaders. For Heldai, Tobijah, and Jedaiah the crowns will be preserved as a memorial in the Temple. Since this is a symbolic act, the crowns are not permanent headpieces for either Zerubbabel or Joshua. Zechariah then predicts that others from far off will come to help in rebuilding the Temple. Are these other Judahites who will come with their wealth and help to rebuild (Petersen), or are they foreigners? Prophesies elsewhere state that foreigners will bring their wealth to the restored Judahite community (Isa 45:16; 60:4–7, 11, 16; 61:5–6; 66:12; Hag 2:7), that foreigners will come to rebuild the walls of Jerusalem (Isa 60:10), and that foreigners will come to worship Yahweh, God of Israel, in Jerusalem (Mic 4:1–2; Isa 45:14; 55:5; 56:3–8; 60:3; Zech 8:22), but not that foreigners will help in rebuilding the Temple. An offer was made previously by the Samaritans to help in the rebuilding, but it was rebuffed (Ezra 4:1–3). When people see others joining in the rebuilding, they will know that Yahweh has sent Zechariah as his prophet (6:15a; cf. 2:9, 11 [Heb. 2:13, 15]; 4:9b). This will happen only if people diligently obey the voice of Yahweh their God (6:15b).

Joshua Also Crowned the Shoot (6:9–15)

REFLECTION

1. We have always assumed the "Shoot" to be a Messianic King in the line of David, elsewhere Zerubbabel but here conferred upon the high priest. Might this explain why people at the time of Jesus did not know for sure who the Messiah was (cf. Mark 8:27–30)? John the Baptist was son of a priest (Luke 1:5).

22

JERUSALEM TO BE CALLED THE FAITHFUL CITY (8:1-8)

8 ¹And the word of Yahweh of hosts came to me: ²Thus said Yahweh of hosts: I am jealous for Zion with great jealousy, and I am jealous for her with great wrath. ³Thus said Yahweh of hosts: I am returning to Zion and will dwell in the midst of Jerusalem, and Jerusalem will be called the faithful city and the mountain of Yahweh of hosts the holy mountain. ⁴Thus said Yahweh of hosts: Old men and old women will again sit in the streets of Jerusalem, each with staff in hand for great age. ⁵And the streets of the city will be full of boys and girls playing in its streets. ⁶Thus said Yahweh of hosts: If it is marvelous in the eyes of the remnant of this people in these days, should it also be marvelous in my eyes, oracle of Yahweh of hosts? ⁷Thus said Yahweh of hosts: Behold I will save my people from the east country and from the west country; ⁸and I will

Jerusalem to Be Called the Faithful City (8:1–8)

bring them to dwell in the midst of Jerusalem;
and they will be my people and I will be their
God—in faithfulness and in righteousness.

RHETORIC AND COMPOSITION

THE PRESENT PASSAGE IS delimited in the Hebrew Bible by sections at top and bottom. Other sections after 8:3, 5, and 6 are presumably placed because subsequent verses contain more divine words from Yahweh. The *BHS*, *BHQ*, and Petersen scan the verses as poetry; the RSV and NRSV take them as prose. Jerusalem being the "faithful city" in 8:3 balances Yahweh's "faithfulness" in 8:8.

MESSAGE

Here begins a series of divine oracles that continue to the end of the chapter. Yahweh begins by saying that he is jealous for Zion with a great jealousy (1:14b); he is also jealous with a great wrath toward her enemies (1:15; cf. Ezek 36:5–6). Yahweh is returning to Zion and will dwell in Jerusalem (1:16b; 2:10 [Heb. 2:14]). Jerusalem will be called the faithful city (Isa 1:26), and Mount Zion will be Yahweh's holy mountain (Jer 31:23; Obad 17; Joel 3:17 [Heb. 4:17]). In this (future) day old men and old women, each with staff in hand, will be seen in the streets of Jerusalem (cf. Isa 65:20), and alongside boys and girls will be playing (8:5; cf. 1 Macc 14:9). After the destruction of Jerusalem old people sat on the ground in silence and young girls bowed their heads to the ground (Lam 2:20). If this new reality will be marvelous in the eyes of the remnant community (Hag 1:12, 14; 2:2), will it (not) also be marvelous in the eyes of Yahweh? Yahweh will save his dispersed people from east and west, bringing them to dwell again in Jerusalem (Jer 30:10–11;

ZECHARIAH

46:27–28; Isa 43:5–6) where they will be his people and he will be their God (Jer 30:22; 31:1, 33)—in faithfulness and in righteousness.

REFLECTION

1. Do we not enjoy seeing old men and women sitting on park benches with young boys and girls playing in the street beside them? What would it be like if our city streets, strewn with rubble, were empty of young and old? It is happening today in countries torn by war.

2. This passage closes with the covenant formula between the Lord and his people, but does not the covenant need to be kept in faithfulness and righteousness?

23

LET YOUR HANDS BE STRONG! (8:9-13)

8 ⁹Thus said Yahweh of hosts: "Let your hands be strong, you who have been hearing in these days these words from the mouth of the prophets that came in the day the foundation of the house of Yahweh of hosts was laid, that the Temple might be built. ¹⁰For before those days there was no wage for human and no wage for beast; neither was there any peace from the foe for one who went out or came in, and I set every person against his fellow. ¹¹But now, not as in the former days, I will not be to the remnant of this people, oracle of Yahweh of hosts. ¹²Indeed there will be a seed of peace; the vine will yield its fruit, and the earth will give its increase, and the heavens will give their dew; and I will cause the remnant of this people to possess all these things. ¹³And it will be as you have been a curse among the nations, O house of Judah and house of Israel, so

will I save you and you will be a blessing. Do not
fear, but let your hands be strong.

RHETORIC AND COMPOSITION

The present passage is delimited in the Hebrew Bible by sections at top and bottom. The *BHS* and Petersen scan 8:9–13, and the *BHQ* 8:10–13 as poetry; the RSV and NRSV take all the verses as prose. The passage begins and ends with this admonition (inclusio):

8:9 Let your hands be strong
8:13 let your hands be strong

"Do not fear" in 8:13 is a catchword to 8:15 in the next oracle.

MESSAGE

Yahweh in this word says to let your hands be strong, i.e., to be of good courage (Hag 2:4; cf. Judg 7:11; Isa 35:3), those of you who have been hearing in these days words from the prophets that came when the foundation of the Temple was laid, which was two years ago, that the rebuilding might be brought to completion. Reference is to the preaching of Haggai and Zechariah's own preaching if he is the speaker here. Before the rebuilding got underway no wages were paid for human or animal work, so meager were the crops (Hag 1:6, 10–11; 2:16–17, 19). Interference came upon everyone from Samaritans up north (Ezra 4:1), not to mention the internal dissention over whether or not to get on with the project (Hag 1:2).

However now, Yahweh will not be to the remnant of his people as in former days. The seed of peace will be sown, the earth will give its increase, the heavens above will give their dew, and the remnant will possess all these things.

Let Your Hands Be Strong! (8:9–13)

People will not have to pray for rain (8:12; cf. Zech 10:1). As the house of Israel and Judah had been a curse among the nations, so now Yahweh will save them, and they will be a blessing. People are not to fear, but to let their hands be strong!

REFLECTION

1. How many times have you read the words "Fear not!" in Scripture. Have those words ever helped you to keep going when the going was rough?

24

SPEAK THE TRUTH, RENDER TRUE JUDGMENTS IN THE GATE! (8:14-17)

8 ¹⁴For thus said Yahweh of hosts: "As I purposed to do evil to you when your fathers provoked me to wrath, said Yahweh of hosts, and I did not relent, ¹⁵so now I have purposed in these days to do good to Jerusalem and to the house of Judah. Do not fear! ¹⁶These are the things you shall do: Speak the truth, each person to his fellow; truth and peaceful judgment you shall render in your gates; ¹⁷do not devise evil in your hearts, each person against his fellow; and do not love a false oath; for all these things I hate, oracle of Yahweh.

Speak the Truth, Render True Judgments in the Gate! (8:14–17)

RHETORIC AND COMPOSITION

THE PRESENT PASSAGE IS delimited at top and bottom by sections in the Hebrew Bible. The *BHS* and *BHQ* scan 8:16–17 and Petersen all of 8:14–17 as poetry; the RSV and NRSV take all the verses as prose. "Do not fear" in 8:15 is a catchword to 8:13 in the prior oracle. "Truth and peace" in 8:16 are catchwords to "truth and peace" in 8:19 of the following oracle.

MESSAGE

Yahweh says here that as he purposed to do evil when Judahite's ancestors provoked him to wrath (1:2; 7:12; Jer 21:5), and he did not relent, so now he purposes to do good to Jerusalem and Judah (Jer 31:28). Do not fear! What are the people to do? Speak the truth, one to another (Ps 15:2); render truth and judgments leading to peace in the city gates (Köhler 1956; cf. 7:9; Deut 25:7; Ruth 4:1, 11; Amos 5:15; Isa 29:21; Job 5:4); do not devise evil in the heart, one person against another; and do not love a false oath (5:4; 7:10; Exod 20:16; 23:7; Deut 5:20; 19:16–19). All these things Yahweh hates (Prov 6:16–19). In an earlier prophecy (7:8–14) Zechariah admonishes people to execute true judgment and show steadfast love and mercy to one another. But the covenant people of earlier times refused to listen (1:4; cf. Jer 6:16–17, 19; 7:13, 26–27; 11:10; 13:11; etc.), turned a stubborn shoulder (Neh 9:29; cf. Hos 4:6), and stopped (lit. made heavy, dulled) their ears from hearing (Isa 6:10; Jer 6:10; 35:17). Their hearts they made like hard rock from hearing the law and Yahweh's words spoken by former prophets (Jer 17:1; Ezek 3:9; 11:19). As a result, they incited the wrath of Yahweh, and the pleasant land they inhabited was made a desolation.

ZECHARIAH

REFLECTION

1. People are told here to speak the truth, each person to his fellow. Is that happening in the world you inhabit?
2. What about speaking the truth and rendering peaceful judgments in the courts? Is that happening in the world you inhabit?

25

FASTS AND FEASTS IN JOY AND GLADNESS (8:18-19)

> 8 ¹⁸And the word of Yahweh of hosts came to me: ¹⁹"Thus said Yahweh of hosts: the fast of the fourth month, and the fast of the fifth month, and the fast of the seventh month, and the fast of the tenth month shall be to the house of Judah for joy and for gladness and for good assemblies. So love truth and peace.

RHETORIC AND COMPOSITION

THE PRESENT PASSAGE IS delimited in the Hebrew Bible by sections at top and bottom. The *BHS* and Petersen scan these verses as poetry; the *BHQ*, the RSV, and the NRSV take them as prose. "Truth and peace" in 8:19 are catchwords to "truth and peace" in 8:16.

MESSAGE

The prophet receives here a word from Yahweh on fasts and pilgrim feasts, supplementing what was said in 7:3–4 about fasts in the fifth and seventh months. Added fasts are in the fourth month and tenth months. On the ninth day of the fourth month the Babylonians made a breach in the walls of Jerusalem (2 Kgs 25:3–5; Jer 52:6–8); the tenth day of the tenth month is when the siege of Jerusalem began (2 Kgs 25:1). "Good assemblies" doubtless occur in the yearly pilgrimage Feasts of Weeks (Pentecost) and Booths (cf. Deut 16:11, 14; Zeph 3:17b–18a). "Joy and gladness" is a favorite Jeremiah word-pair (Jer 7:34; 15:16; 16:9; 25:10; 33:11, 13), occurring also in Isa 22:13; 35:10; 51:3, 11; and Ps 51:8 [Heb. 51:10]. The prophet closes: "So love truth and peace" (cf. 8:16). Love in the OT can be commanded (Deut 6:4–5; Amos 5:15; Ps 31:23 [Heb. 31:24]).

REFLECTION

1. Here people are told they can fast on designated days, but they are to do so in joy and gladness. Is there joy and gladness in your Christmas and Easter celebrations, also on other festive occasions?

26

MANY WILL SEEK YAHWEH'S FAVOR IN JERUSALEM (8:20-23)

8 ²⁰Thus said Yahweh of hosts: Peoples shall yet come, yes, the inhabitants of many cities; ²¹the inhabitants of one city shall go to another, saying, "Let us indeed go to entreat the face of Yahweh and to seek Yahweh of hosts. Let me go also!" ²²Many peoples and strong nations will come to seek Yahweh of hosts in Jerusalem and go to entreat the face of Yahweh. ²³Thus said Yahweh of hosts: In those days ten men will grab hold, from all tongues of the nations, and will grab hold of the corner of the skirt of each Judahite, saying, "Let us go with you, for we have heard that God is with you."

RHETORIC AND COMPOSITION

THE PRESENT PASSAGE IS delimited at top and bottom by sections in the Hebrew Bible. Another section occurs after 8:22, perhaps because 8:23 is taken to be a concluding word from Yahweh. With this verse the prophecies of Zechariah are ended. The *BHS*, *BHQ*, and Petersen scan 8:20–22 as poetry; the RSV and NRSV take the verses as prose. The speaker nicely inverts the following expressions:

8:21	*to entreat* the face of Yahweh
	and *to seek* Yahweh
8:22	*to seek* Yahweh
	to entreat the face of Yahweh

This repetition occurs at the beginning and end of the passage (inclusio):

| 8:20 | Let us indeed go ... |
| 8:23 | Let us go ... |

MESSAGE

Zechariah concludes his words of hope and prosperity for the remnant community by first repeating the theme that people from all nations will come to Jerusalem to entreat and worship Yahweh (Mic 4:1–2; Isa 2:2–3; Isa 56:3–8; 60:3). There is a sense of urgency in this prophecy, borne out by key repetitions. In 8:21 another voice interrupts, "*Let me go* also!" In a possible add-on verse *ten men will grab hold*, from all languages of the nations, and *will grab hold* of the corner of the skirt of each Judahite and say, "*Let us* go with you, for we have heard that God is with you" (cf. Isa 45:14b; 55:5). "God with us" (Emmanuel), spoken earlier by Isaiah (Isa 7:14), becomes the name of Jesus the Christ (Matt 1:23).

Many Will Seek Yahweh's Favor in Jerusalem (8:20–23)

REFLECTION

1. Is your worship as Christians and your personal life in the Lord such that others from outside might urgently want to join you?

II.
ZECHARIAH

27

JUDGMENT AGAINST SYRIA, PHOENICIA, AND THE PHILISTINES (9:1-8)

9 ¹An oracle. The word of Yahweh against the land of Hadrak
    and against Damascus, its resting place
For to Yahweh belongs the eye of all humanity
    and all the tribes of Israel
²Also Hamath that borders on her
    Tyre and Sidon, because she is very wise[1]
³Yes, Tyre has built herself a fortification
    and heaped up silver like dust
        and gold like mud of the streets
⁴Behold, the Lord will dispossess her
    and hurl her wealth into the sea
        and she shall be devoured by fire
⁵Ashkelon will see and be afraid
    Gaza, too, shall writhe violently
        and Ekron, for her hope will wither

---

1. LXX has "they are very wise."

> Yes, the king from Gaza will perish
>   and Ashkelon will not be inhabited
> ⁶A mongrel people will dwell in Ashdod
>   and I will cut off the pride of the Philistines
> ⁷And I will take away his blood from his mouth
>   and his detested things from between his teeth
> But he also will be a remnant for our God
>   and he will be like a clan-chief in Judah
>   and Ekron like the Jebusite
> ⁸Then I will encamp around my house against any army
>   so no one passes through or returns
> No oppressor shall again overrun them
>   for now I see with my eyes.

RHETORIC AND COMPOSITION

THIS PASSAGE IS DELIMITED by sections in the Hebrew Bible. The *BHS* and *BHQ* take the verses as prose, but the RSV and NRSV scan them as poetry. A nice chiasmus exists in 9:5:

> Ashkelon ...
>   Gaza ...
>   Ekron ...
>   Gaza ...
> Ashkelon ...

A keyword ties-in beginning and end:

9:1   For to Yahweh belongs *the eye* of all humanity

9:8   for now I see with *my eyes*.

MESSAGE

Chs. 9–11 are designated an oracle from Yahweh (cf. 12:1; Hag 1:1). 9:1–8 is Yahweh's judgment upon Syria,

Judgment against Syria, Phoenicia, and the Philistines (9:1–8)

Phoenicia, and the Philistines, their depopulated territory then being incorporated into Judah. Hadrak is a region north of Palestine, named by Tiglath-pileser III (745–727) in the Assyrian documents as Hatarikka, one of the nineteen districts belonging to Hamath ($ANET^3$ 282–83); it was located between Damascus and Hamath. Damascus will be Yahweh's resting place. Yahweh has an eye on all humanity, as well as on all the tribes of Israel. Tyre and Sidon, southernmost cities of Phoenicia (modern Lebanon), said to be very wise (cf. Ezek 28:3–4), will also be added to Yahweh's domain. Tyre and Sidon had built impressive fortifications on the Mediterranean and amassed great wealth (Ezek 27). Tyre was besieged by the Assyrians for five years and could not be taken; Nebuchadnezzar besieged it for thirteen years and was unable to take the city (Mitchell: 265). Alexander the Great, however, took Tyre in seven months in 332, making a causeway between the island and the mainland so he could bring his engines against the city's walls (Mitchell: 266). A wordplay in Hebrew exists between "fortification" (*māṣôr*) and "Tyre" (*ṣôr*). Yahweh will hurl Tyre's wealth into the sea, and the city itself will be devoured by fire. Four cities of the Philistines will see and be afraid (9:5). They, too, will be uninhabited. Gath, the fifth Philistine city, is no longer in existence. Sargon II of Assyria claims to have conquered the city in his campaign against Ashdod in 711 ($ANET^3$ 286; cf. Isa 20; Jer 25:20), and destruction may have come earlier (cf. Amos 1:6–8).

A half-breed people will inhabit Ashdod (9:6). But Yahweh will take the idolatrous sacrifices (with blood) out of its mouth (cf. Ezek 33:25). Israelites were forbidden to eat the blood (Deut 12:16, 23–24; Lev 17:10–14; cf. 1 Sam 13:31–34). The "detested things" were probably animals, fish, and fowl forbidden by Mosaic law (Deut 14:3–21). But then, even from this mongrel people that inhabits Philistia

II. ZECHARIAH

will come a remnant who will worship Yahweh and be incorporated into Judah. Jebusites were the old inhabitants of Jerusalem, conquered but not destroyed by David (2 Sam 5:6–9; 1 Kgs 9:20). Yahweh will protect his land and Jerusalem so no unwelcome oppressor will pass through, where "house" refers here to the Holy Land (Mitchell: 269; cf. Hos 9:15; Jer 12:7). Yahweh will oversee his territory with his own eyes.

REFLECTION

1. David subdued the Philistines (2 Sam 5:17–25; 8:1), won a victory as far as the Euphrates (2 Sam 8:3–8) and subdued the Syrians (2 Sam 10:15–19); Solomon was sovereign over kingdoms from the Euphrates to the land of the Philistines (1 Kgs 4:21 [Heb. 5:1]); and Jeroboam II expanded northern Israelite territory into Syria (2 Kgs 14:25). Do you think the present prediction of an expanded Israel was ever fulfilled?

2. Do you know why the Israelites were forbidden to eat the blood? See Lev 17:10–11, 14; Deut 12:23.

28

MESSIANIC KING ENTERS ZION IN TRIUMPH (9:9-17)

9 ⁹Rejoice greatly, O Daughter Zion!
  shout aloud, O Daughter Jerusalem!
Behold, your king comes to you
  righteous and victorious is he
Humble and riding on a donkey
  on a colt, the foal of a donkey
¹⁰And I will cut off the chariot from Ephraim
  and the horse from Jerusalem
And the battle bow will be cut off
  and he will speak peace to the nations
And his dominion will be from sea to sea
  and from the River to the ends of the earth.
¹¹You also, because of the blood of your covenant,
  I have set your prisoners free
    out of the waterless pit
¹²Return to the stronghold
  prisoners of hope
Also today a declaration:

II. ZECHARIAH

> I will restore double to you
> ¹³For I have bent Judah for me
> > I have filled Ephraim the bow
> And I will arouse your sons, O Zion
> > against your sons, O Javan[1]
> > > and make you as the sword of a mighty man
> ¹⁴Then Yahweh will be seen over them
> > and his arrow will go forth like the lightning
> And the Lord Yahweh will blow the trumpet
> > and march in the whirlwinds of the south
> ¹⁵Yahweh of hosts will defend them
> > and they will devour and tread down thesling stones
> And they will drink, be boisterous as with wine
> > and they will be filled like a bowl
> > > like the corners of the altar
> ¹⁶And Yahweh their God will save them
> > in that day, as the flock of his people
> Indeed, stones of a crown
> > lifted high upon his land
> ¹⁷Indeed how great the goodness, how great his beauty!
> > grain shall make the young men flourish
> > > and new wine the young women.

RHETORIC AND COMPOSITION

THESE VERSES ARE DELIMITED at the top end by a section in the Hebrew Bible, and at the bottom end by the chapter division. The verses are scanned in the *BHS*, *BHQ*, RSV, and NRSV as poetry. Toward the end of the passage are some nice repetitions beginning the lines:

9:11   You *also* . . .

9:12   *Also* today . . .

---

1. Hebrew name for Ionia, i.e., Greece (cf. Gen 10:2, 4).

Messianic King Enters Zion in Triumph (9:9–17)

9:16   *Indeed . . .*
9:17   *Indeed how . . . and how . . .*

MESSAGE

In this passage the Messianic King enters Jerusalem in triumph, bringing peace to the nations and to Judahites still in exile. The coming of the Messiah is greeted by people with acclaim and great rejoicing (cf. Zech 2:10 [Heb. 2:13]; Zeph 3:14–15). This king is righteous (cf Isa 11:3–5; 16:6; 32:1; Jer 23:5; 33:15) and victorious (cf. Ps 33:16), humble and riding on a donkey (cf. Jer 22:4). From earliest times Israelites—even kings—rode upon donkeys (Gen 49:10–11; Judg 10:4; 12:14; 2 Sam 16:2), so one need not expect the king to be riding on a horse.

Yahweh intervenes to say that he will cut off the chariot from Ephraim, i.e., North Israel (cf. Hos 4:17; 5:3, 5, 9; Jer 31:6, 9, 18, 20), and the horse from Jerusalem (Mic 5:10 [Heb. 5:9]), and that his king will speak peace to the nations (Isa 2:4 (=Mic 4:3); 9:6 [Heb. 9:5]). The entire land will be demilitarized. Northern Israel will be occupied by its former inhabitants (9:12; 10:6–7; Jer 3:12, 18; 31:2–9, 15–20). This Messianic King will reign from sea to sea, i.e., from the Mediterranean to some sea in the distant east (not the Dead Sea), and from the River, i.e., the Euphrates (Deut 11:24; Josh 1:4; Jer 2:18), to the ends of the earth (Ps 72:8).

Addressing Daughter Zion in Babylon, Yahweh says he will set prisoners free from their captivity. They have been in waterless pits. Driver thinks the prisoners may have died there from thirst, but the prisoners could also have drowned if the pits contained water. Why the release? Because of Yahweh's covenant with the nation sealed by blood (Exod 24:5–8). These prisoners with hope now of deliverance are encouraged to return to their "stronghold," which may be

II. ZECHARIAH

Zion, because of a wordplay between the two terms "stronghold" and "Zion" (Petersen). Yahweh has this declaration to make: he will restore to the prisoners double, where "double" means equivalent compensation or compensation in full measure (cf. Jer 16:18; 17:18; Isa 40:2; Rev 18:6; Lundbom 1999: 771).

In 9:13–15, language shifts from disarmament and peace to warfare; the actor is Yahweh. Yahweh will bring about a dramatic victory over the Greeks; Judah will be his bow and Ephraim his arrows. Yahweh himself will be seen—in a great storm, a blowing of the trumpet (thunder?) and a marching in the whirlwind. Yahweh's people will be able to devour the enemy and tread down sling stones hurled against them, then drink the blood of their enemies as wine in boisterous celebration. Drinking enemy blood is not to be taken literally (Petersen). Blood in bowls will be tossed against the four sides of the altar (Exod 24:6–8; Lev 1:5, 11). Yahweh will save his people as a shepherd saves his flock. They will be crown jewels upon his land. The passage closes by celebrating the goodness and beauty of the land once warfare is ended, citing two of the most valued gifts of the soil: grain for the young men and new wine for the young women.

Fulfillment of 9:9 comes with Jesus's ride into Jerusalem on Palm Sunday (Matt 21:1–9; Mark 11:1–10; Luke 19:29–38; John 12:12–15), although Matthew misreads the Hebrew parallelism in 9:9 by imagining both a donkey and colt secured for the ride. Jesus will ride only on one animal!

Handel's *Messiah* oratorio incorporates portions of two verses from this prophecy:

Messiah Part 1

Movement 18: Zech 9:9–10

Messianic King Enters Zion in Triumph (9:9–17)

> Rejoice greatly, O daughter of Zion! Shout, O daughter of Jerusalem! Behold, thy King cometh unto thee! He is the righteous Saviour, and He shall speak peace unto the heathen.

REFLECTION

1. Do you think another Messianic King was imagined to be riding into Jerusalem in Zechariah's day? If so, was Jesus another kind of king bringing in another kind of kingdom?
2. Did Jesus bring peace to the nations, as 9:10 envisions? See Luke 2:14 and Matt 10:34–36.
3. Three other prophets refer to dealings with Greece? Can you name one? For the answer see the end of Malachi.

29

IN YAHWEH'S NAME SHALL PEOPLE WALK ABOUT (10:3-12)

10 ³Against the shepherds my anger burns hot
    and against the male goats I will visit
For Yahweh of hosts has visited his flock
    the house of Judah
        and will make them as his stately horse in battle
⁴From him the cornerstone
    from him the tent peg
From him the battle bow
    from him will come forth every ruler together
⁵And they will be as mighty men in battle
    treading down (the foe) in the mud of the streets
        in battle
They shall fight because Yahweh is with them
    and riders on horses shall be put to shame
⁶And I will strengthen the house of Judah
    and the house of Joseph I will save
And I will bring them back, for I have compassion on them
    and they will be as though I had not rejected them

In Yahweh's Name Shall People Walk About (10:3–12)

>   for I am Yahweh their God, and I will answer them
> ⁷Then Ephraim will be as mighty men
>   and their heart will be glad as with wine
> Their children shall see and be glad
>   their heart shall rejoice in Yahweh
> ⁸I will whistle to them and I will gather them in
>   for I have redeemed them
>   and they will increase as they increased
> ⁹And though I scattered them among the peoples
>   yet in far countries they shall remember me
>   and they shall be with their children and return
> ¹⁰I will bring them back from the land of Egypt
>   and from Assyria I will gather them
> And to the land of Gilead and to Lebanon I will bring them
>   so (no place) will be found for them
> ¹¹And he will pass through the sea of distress
>   and he will smite the waves in the sea
>   and all the depths of the Nile will dry up
> The pride of Assyria will be brought down
>   and the rod of Egypt will depart
> ¹²And I will make them strong in Yahweh
>   and in his name shall they walk about
>   oracle of Yahweh.

RHETORIC AND COMPOSITION

THESE VERSES ARE DELIMITED in the Hebrew Bible by sections at top and bottom. In conclusion is an "oracle of Yahweh" formula. The passage is poetry. "Shepherds" in 10:3 is a link term back to "shepherd" in 10:2, and "Lebanon" in 10:10 is a link term to "Lebanon" in 11:1. A fourfold repetition of "out" exists in 10:4 (anaphora), and in 10:4 is this repetition:

> ⁴*From him* . . .
>   *from him* . . .
> *From him* . . .
>   *from him* will come forth . . .

II. ZECHARIAH

Numerous syntactic chiasms also appear in the passage (6a; 10a; 11c; 12a).

MESSAGE

The passage begins with a play on the verb "visit": Yahweh will *visit* the he-goats (foreign rulers; cf. Isa 14:9; Ezek 34:17) to punish, but *has visited* his own flock, the house of Judah, to deliver it from oppression (1:14–15; 8:2). The second occurrence, "has visited," is a prophetic perfect, i.e., "will visit." Shepherds in 10:3 are also foreign rulers (cf. Jer 25:34–38; Nah 3:18). Yahweh will make Judah like a stately horse in battle (cf. Job 39:19–25). From Judah will come the cornerstone, the tent peg, the battle bow, and every ruler together. "Cornerstone" is used to describe princes or leading men in Judg 20:2; 1 Sam 14:38; and Isa 19:13. The "tent peg" supports the state and the "battle bow" is the implement of war (cf. 9:13). Tg interprets these images to refer to the "Anointed One," i.e., the Messiah. All will be as mighty men in battle, trampling the enemy in the mud of the streets (cf. Mic 7:10; Ps 18:42 [Heb. 18:43]). Yahweh will be with them in the fight, and enemy riders on horses will be put to shame (cf. Ezek 23:6, 12, 23; 38:15).

Yahweh will strengthen Judah and save the house of Joseph, i.e., Northern Israelites still in exile. Ephraim, here also a name for North Israel (9:10, 13; 10:7; Hos 4:17; 5:3, 5; etc.), was a son of Joseph (Gen 48:1). Yahweh will bring exiles back and have compassion on them, where "have compassion" is another prophetic perfect. It will be as though Yahweh had not rejected them. Yahweh is their God and will answer them. Ephraim will be as mighty men; their heart made glad as with wine (cf. Ps 104:15; Eccl 10:19). Their children shall see and be glad. Yahweh will whistle for them, as a shepherd whistles for his flock (Judg 5:16; cf.

Isa 5:26; 7:18), and gather them in, and they will increase in numbers as before. Though Yahweh scattered them, yet in these faraway places they will remember Yahweh, will rear their children and then return (cf. Jer 29:6). They will come from Egypt and Assyria, returning to Gilead in Transjordan from where Tiglath-pileser III exiled them in 733. Gilead was a core land of the northern kingdom (Deut 3:8–20; *pace* Boda: 630). Zechariah also envisions them coming to inhabit Lebanon, which is a stretch! But see Obad 20. Zechariah is given to more hyperbole in saying no room will exist anywhere for all the returnees (cf. Isa 49:20; 54:1–3).

Yahweh will pass through a distressed sea and smite the waves so a path will be made for people to cross, just as he did at the Red Sea (Exod 14:21–22; cf. Isa 11:15; 43:2). The pride of Assyria will be brought low (cf. Isa 10:12–14). Egypt's rod, an emblem of oppression (Isa 9:4 [Heb. 9:3]), will depart. Yahweh closes by saying he will give his people might in himself, and in his name shall they walk about.

REFLECTION

1. Male goats are here a negative image and sheep a positive one. Might this distinction carry over into the NT? See Matt 25:32–33.

2. Jeremiah and Ezekiel prophesied that one day people of North Israel would be united with people of Judah (Jer 31:1–20; Ezek 37:15–28). Did Northern Israelites exiled to Assyrian and Median cities in 733 and 722 ever return, either to Samaria or Zion? Today we speak of the "10 lost tribes of the Northern Kingdom."

3. When were Judahites taken to Egypt in exile? Might some have fled on their own when Nebuchadnezzar and the Babylonians came to Jerusalem in 598 and 586?

II. ZECHARIAH

4. What might it mean today to walk about in the name of the Lord?

30

WOE TO THE WORTHLESS SHEPHERD! (11: 4-17)

⁴Thus said Yahweh my God: Shepherd the flock doomed to slaughter, ⁵whose buyers kill them and are not held guilty, and those selling them say, "Blessed be Yahweh, for I have become rich." Yes, their own shepherds have no pity on them. ⁶For I will no longer have pity on the inhabitants of the earth, oracle of Yahweh. But behold, I will cause everyone, each person, to fall into the hand of his neighbor and into the hand of his king, and they shall beat to pieces the people of earth, and I will not deliver from their hand.

⁷So I shepherded the flock doomed to slaughter, truly the poor of the flock. And I took for myself two staffs, the one I called Pleasant and the other I called Bind, and I shepherded the flock. ⁸And I destroyed the three shepherds in one month, for I myself became impatient with them, also they themselves loathed me. ⁹So

II. ZECHARIAH

I said, "I will not shepherd you; what is to die, let it die, and what is to be destroyed, let it be destroyed; and let those that remain devour the flesh of one another!" ¹⁰I took my staff Pleasant and I broke it to break the covenant that I had cut with all the peoples. ¹¹So it was broken in that day, thus the poor of the flock who were watching me knew that it was the word of Yahweh. ¹²Then I said to them, "If it is good in your eyes, give me my wages; and if not, hold back." So they weighed out my wages, thirty shekels of silver. ¹³Then Yahweh said to me, "Throw them to the potter"[1]—this noble price at which I was valued by them! So I took the thirty shekels of silver and threw them to the potter in the house of Yahweh. ¹⁴Then I broke my second staff, Bind, breaking the family ties between Judah and Israel.

¹⁵Then Yahweh said to me: Take again for yourself the implements of a worthless shepherd. ¹⁶For behold, I am raising up a shepherd in the land who will not visit the youth, seek the wandering, not heal the maimed, not nourish, but the flesh of the fat ones he will devour, tearing their hoofs in pieces.

¹⁷Woe to the worthless shepherd
   who deserts the flock!
May the sword be upon his arm
   and upon his right eye!
Let his arm be completely withered
   and his right eye utterly blinded!

---

1. MT reads "potter"; the RSV and NRSV following Greek α', Vg, and the Pesh read "treasury," considering the word's repetition concluding the verse.

Woe to the Worthless Shepherd! (11: 4–17)

RHETORIC AND COMPOSITION

THESE VERSES ARE DELIMITED by sections in the Hebrew Bible; 11:4–16 is prose and 11:17 poetry. But Petersen scans all of 11:4–17 as poetry. Two additional section markings occur after 11:14 and 16. "Shepherd(s)" in 11:4–17 is a link term back to "shepherds" in 11:3. The genre of this passage is difficult to determine. Driver calls it an allegory, although he says it is obscure, not having an interpretation. Mitchell calls it a parable; Petersen a symbolic action and Boda prophetic sign-acts (the same as symbolic acts) used to communicate an allegory.

MESSAGE

This passage prophesies the doom of worthless shepherds Judahites have allowed to rule them. Yahweh begins by telling the prophet to shepherd a flock readied for market. Current buyers have been killing them and are not held guilty, and current sellers bless Yahweh because they have become rich (11:4–5). Buyers and sellers are said by some to be Persian or Greek overlords, but more likely they are Judahite leaders, for the prophet goes on to say that the people's own shepherds have no pity on them (11:5). This being the case, Yahweh will no longer have pity on the inhabitants of earth. His judgment has enormous consequences: Every person will fall into the hand of either his neighbor or his king, and the earth will experience massive destruction. Yahweh will do nothing to deliver the victims (11:6).

So, the prophet assumed his task over the doomed flock, the poor flock, taking for himself two staffs, one called Pleasant and the other Bind, and shepherded the flock. In one month he destroyed three shepherds over the people. He became impatient with them, and they loathed him, so he left the sheep to their fate. Let those die, die, those to be

II. ZECHARIAH

destroyed, be destroyed, and those who remain to consume one another in conflict.

The prophet then breaks his first staff, Pleasant, annulling the covenant made between Yahweh and the peoples. This was apparently a covenant of peace Yahweh made with other nations (Driver; cf. Hos 2:18 [Heb. 2:20]; Ezek 34:25). The poor flock, who is watching this symbolic act, knows then that the prophet eancts the word of Yahweh.

The prophet then asks fellow Judahites for his wages, and they weigh out for him a paltry thirty shekels of silver, the value of a Hebrew slave gored by an ox (Exod 21:32). But the prophet has done a poor job of shepherding the flock. Disgusted with the amount, the prophet throws the noble sum to the potter in the Temple. Who was this potter? Probably someone making pottery vessels, perhaps even idols (cf. 13:2). The prophet then breaks his second staff, Bind, breaking the family ties between Israel and Judah. By breaking both staffs, the prophet shows he will have nothing more to do with this people.

In a supplemental word Yahweh tells the prophet to take again for himself a staff, a club, a pouch, and perhaps a pipe for whistling to the sheep (1 Sam 17:40; Judg 5:16). He is to be a sign to the people that Yahweh is raising up a shepherd who will not look after the youth, will not seek out the wandering, will not heal the maimed (cf. Ezek 34:16), will not nourish, but will instead eat the fat ones of the flock, tearing even their hoofs in pieces.

The passage closes with a poetic verse casting woe on the worthless shepherd who deserts his flock (cf. John 10:12). May his arm be completely withered and his right eye blinded! For other depictions of bad or worthless shepherds, see Ezek 34:1–6 and Isa 56:11–12. This poetry is like the poetry in 13:7–9, where the shepherd is smitten and the flock scattered. There two-thirds of the flock perish and

Woe to the Worthless Shepherd! (11: 4–17)

one-third will be kept alive. Those surviving will be refined in the fiery furnace, after which they will call upon Yahweh's name. The covenant will be reaffirmed.

In the NT 11:13 is quoted after Judas throws on the Temple floor the thirty shekels of silver he had received for betraying Jesus; the chief priests and elders refuse to deposit the money in the Temple treasury. After further consultation, the money is used to buy the potter's field to bury foreigners (Matt 27:3–10; cf. 26:15). Matthew mistakenly attributes the prophecy to Jeremiah, although other ancient authorities read Zechariah.

REFLECTION

1. Judahites had good leadership under Zerubbabel the governor and Joshua the high priest, but is it not possible that other leaders during the Persian period were sorely inadequate? Does it not happen also in modern states?
2. Will the broken ties between Israel and Judah last?

31

YAHWEH WILL FIRST GIVE VICTORY TO JUDAH (12:7-14)

12 ⁷And Yahweh will save the tents of Judah first, that the boasting of the house of David and the boasting of the inhabitants of Jerusalem may not be greater than that of Judah. ⁸In that day Yahweh will defend the inhabitants of Jerusalem, and it will be that he who stumbles among them will, in that day, be as David, and the house of David will be as God, as the angel of Yahweh, before them. ⁹And it will be in that day that I will seek to destroy all the nations that come against Jerusalem.

¹⁰And I will pour out upon the house of David and upon the inhabitants of Jerusalem a spirit of grace and supplication, and they will look upon me whom they have pierced, and they will mourn for him as one mourns for an only child, and weep bitterly over him as one weeps over a firstborn. ¹¹In that day the mourning in

Yahweh Will First Give Victory to Judah (12:7–14)

Jerusalem will be as great as the Hadad-rimmon mourning in the plain of Megiddo. ¹²The land shall mourn, each family by itself; the family of the house of David by itself, and their wives by themselves; the family of Nathan by itself, and their wives by themselves; ¹³the family of Levi by itself, and their wives by themselves; the family of the Shimeites by itself, and their wives by themselves; ¹⁴and all the families that are left, each by itself, and their wives by themselves.

RHETORIC AND COMPOSITION

THE PRESENT PASSAGE IS delimited by sections in the Hebrew Bible, and is prose. But Petersen scans the verses as poetry. The "in that day" repetitions in 12:8 (2x), 9, and 11 are a link to the repetitions of "in that day" in 12:3, 4, and 6. More "in that day" repetitions occur in 13:1, 2, and 4. "They have pierced" in 12:10 is also a link term to "shall pierce him" in 13:3.

MESSAGE

In this passage the prophet reports Yahweh as saying that he will first save the tents of Judah so that Jerusalem, in its boast to be the city of David, does not exalt itself over the rest of Judah. "Tents" is an archaic term for dwellings (Jer 4:20; 10:20; 30:18), surviving from nomadic life (Jer 49:29; Hab 3:7). Any schism existing between members of the Davidic line in Jerusalem and the rest of Judah is not known. Yahweh is quick to add that he is nevertheless prepared to defend the inhabitants of Jerusalem (cf. Isa 31:4–5). The feeblest among them will be as strong as David, and the house of David will play the role of God (Boda: 709; cf. Exod 4:16), or, better, will be an angel of Yahweh (cf. 2 Sam

II. ZECHARIAH

14:17), before them—perhaps the other nations. Hyperbole is used to stress the point. Yahweh in that day will destroy all nations that come against Jerusalem (cf. 12:3–4).

Yahweh will pour out upon the house of David and all Jerusalem a spirit of grace and supplication, i.e., prayers for grace or favor, the latter requesting forgiveness for the sin they have committed. People will then look upon the one whom they have pierced, i.e., put to death by the sword, and will mourn bitterly for him. The MT has "look upon *me* whom they have pierced."[1] Has Yahweh (metaphorically) been wounded by the people's rebellion and ingratitude (so Driver; Boda: 717)? Or is reference here to the prophet Zechariah son of Berechiah, who was put to death (Matt 23:29–35; cf. Zech 1:1)? I opt for the latter, taking the speaker here to be assuming the persona of Zechariah. Mourning for the martyr, in any case, will be compared to loud wailing over the death of an only child (cf. Jer 6:26), or to the death of a firstborn (cf. Mic 6:7), or to the Hadad-rimmon mourning in the plain of Megiddo. The last-mentioned mourning is best taken as the mourning over Josiah, who was killed by Phaorah Neco at Megiddo in 609 (2 Kgs 23:29–30; 2 Chr 35:22–25), where Hadad-rimmon would be a place-name at or near Megiddo.

According to 12:13–14, the entire land will mourn: the family of David (descendants of the Davidic line of kings), the family of Nathan (descendants of Nathan, born to one of David's concubine wives; cf. 2 Sam 5:14; Luke 3:31), the family of Levi (descendants of Levi the priest; cf. Deut 10:8), the family of the Shimeites (descendants of Levi's grandson Gershon; cf. Num 3:18, 21), and all remaining families. Wives of the families will mourn separately.

Zech 12:10 is cited in John 19:34–37 as applying to Jesus on the cross, and in Matt 23:29–35 it refers to the

---

1. The RSV corrects to "him," the NRSV to "the one."

Yahweh Will First Give Victory to Judah (12:7–14)

murder of Zechariah (grand)son of Iddo between the sanctuary and the altar.

REFLECTION

1. Do you think a tie-in exists between the words of this prophet in 12:10 to the murder of Zechariah son of Barachiah in Matthew 23?

32

A FOUNTAIN FOR THE CLEANSING OF JERUSALEM (13:1-6)

13 ¹In that day there will be a fountain opened for the house of David and the inhabitants of Jerusalem for sin and for uncleanness. ²And it will be in that day, oracle of Yahweh of hosts, I will cut off the names of the idols from the land, and they shall be remembered no more; also, the prophets and the spirit of uncleanness I will cause to pass out of the land. ³And it will be when anyone will again prophesy, his father and his mother who bore him will say to him, "You shall not live, for you speak lies in the name of Yahweh," and his father and his mother who bore him shall pierce him when he prophesies. ⁴And it will be in that day that the prophets—every one of them—will be ashamed of his vision when he prophesies, and he will not put on a hairy mantle in order

A Fountain for the Cleansing of Jerusalem (13:1–6)

to deceive, ⁵but will say, "I am no prophet, I am a tiller of the soil; for I have been made to possess the land since my youth." ⁶And if one says to him, "What are these wounds between your arms?" Then he will say, "They are those when I was smitten in the house of my friends."

RHETORIC AND COMPOSITION

THIS PASSAGE IS DELIMITED by sections in the Hebrew Bible, and is prose. Petersen, however, scans the verses as poetry. More "in that day" repetitions in 13:1, 2, and 4 link this passage to prior ones. "Shall pierce him" in 13:3 is a link back to "they have pierced" in 12:10.

MESSAGE

The prophet here has another positive word for the Judahites: a fountain will be opened for those with Davidic lineage and the remainder of Jerusalem's population, in order to cleanse them from sin and uncleanness (Zech 3:9; cf. Ezek 36:17, 25; 37:23), where reference is to idols and to prophets prophesying by them. Yahweh will cut off the names of idols (Hos 2:17 [Heb. 2:19]) and pretending prophets from the land, and they will be remembered no more. If any such prophet prophesies, his mother and father shall see to it that he be put to death, for he is speaking lies in the name of Yahweh (cf. Deut 13:1–10 [Heb. 13:2–11]; 21:18–21). In that day prophets not called into service by Yahweh will be ashamed of their visions; they will not put on a hairy mantle to deceive people (cf. 1 Kgs 19:13, 19; 2 Kgs 1:8; 2:8, 13), but will say "I am not a prophet, but have been a tiller of the soil since my youth." If they see telltale wounds on his back, he will say he received them in the house of friends!

II. ZECHARIAH

REFLECTION

1. Do you think John the Baptist's garment of camel's hair (Matt 3:4; Mark 1:6) identified him as a prophet? Elijah the same?
2. Don't mothers and fathers today typically defend their children even when they are engaged in wrongdoing? Should they? If they do not, what then should they do?

33

A DAY OF YAHWEH IS COMING (14:1-21)

14 ¹Behold, a day of Yahweh is coming when your spoil will be divided in your midst. ²Yes, I will gather all the nations to Jerusalem for battle, and the city will be taken, and the houses plundered, and the women ravished; and half of the city will go into exile, but the rest of the people will not be cut off from the city. ³Then Yahweh will go forth and fight against those nations as a day when he fights, in a day of war. ⁴In that day his feet will stand on the Mount of Olives that lies before Jerusalem on the east; and the Mount of Olives will split in half from sunrise to seaward by a very great valley; and half of the Mount will shift northward and the other half southward. ⁵And you will flee to the valley of my mountains, for the valley of my mountains will reach to Azel. Yes, you will flee as you fled from before the earthquake in the days of Uzziah king

II. ZECHARIAH

of Judah. Then Yahweh my God will come, all the holy ones with you.[1]

⁶And it will be in that day there will be no light, neither cold nor frost;[2] ⁷and it will be singular day, known to Yahweh, no day and no night; and it will be at evening time there will be light; ⁸and it will be in that day living waters will go out from Jerusalem, half of them to the eastern sea and half of them to the western sea; in summer and in winter it will be. ⁹And Yahweh will be king over all the earth; in that day it will be that Yahweh will be one and his name one.

¹⁰The whole land will become as the Arabah, from Geba to Rimmon south of Jerusalem. But (Jerusalem) will be lifted up and dwell upon her place, from the Gate of Benjamin to the place of the First Gate, to the Corner Gate, and from the Tower of Hananel to the king's wine vats. ¹¹And they will dwell in her, and there will be no more ban; and Jerusalem will dwell in security.

¹²And this will be the plague with which Yahweh will plague all the peoples that wage war against Jerusalem: its flesh shall rot while it stands upon on its feet, and its eyes shall rot in their sockets, and its tongue shall rot in their mouths. ¹³In that day a great panic from Yahweh will be among them, so each person will lay hold of the hand of his fellow, and his hand will be raised up against the hand of his fellow; ¹⁴yes, even Judah will fight against Jerusalem. And the wealth of all the nations roundabout will be gathered, gold and silver and garments in great abundance. ¹⁵And thus will be the plague of the horse, the mule, the camel, and the ass, and all the beasts that will be in those camps as this plague.

1. The RSV and NRSV correct to "with him."
2. Reading the Qere for this second word.

A Day of Yahweh is Coming (14:1–21)

¹⁶And it will be that everyone who remains from all the nations who have come against Jerusalem that they will go up from year to year to worship the King, Yahweh of hosts, and to keep the Feast of Booths. ¹⁷And it will be if any of the families of the earth do not go up to Jerusalem to worship the King, Yahweh of hosts, that rain will not come upon them. ¹⁸And if the family of Egypt does not go up and comes not, will there not come upon them the plague with which Yahweh plagues the nations that do not go up to keep the Feast of Booths? ¹⁹This shall be the punishment to Egypt and the punishment to all the nations that do not go up to keep the Feast of Booths.
²⁰And in that day there will be upon the bells of the horses, "Holy to Yahweh," and the pots in the house of Yahweh will be as the bowls before the altar; ²¹and every pot in Jerusalem and in Judah will be holy to Yahweh of hosts, and all who sacrifice will come and take from them and boil in them. And there will no longer be a Canaanite in the house of Yahweh of hosts in that day.

RHETORIC AND COMPOSITION

THESE VERSES ARE DELIMITED at the top end by a section in the Hebrew Bible before 14:1; 14:21 is the end of II Zechariah and the book of Zechariah. The passage is taken as prose in the RSV and NRSV, but *BHS* and *BHQ* scan 14:1–4a, 5b–9, 11, and 13 as poetry. The *BHS* also scans 14:14–16 as poetry. Petersen scans all the verses as poetry. More repetitions of "in that day" follow up on "day of Yahweh" in 14:1. The concluding "in that day" in 14:21 makes an inclusio with "day of Yahweh" in 14:1. "Horses" in 14:20 may also make an inclusio with "horse" in 12:4, which begins Oracle II.

II. ZECHARIAH

12:6–9 contains these repetitions:

⁶And it will be in that day . . .
⁷and it will be . . .
and it will be . . .
⁸and it will be in that day . . .
half of them . . .
half of them . . .
. . . it will be
⁹and Yahweh will be . . .
in that day Yahweh will be . . .

MESSAGE

This passage anticipates a day of Yahweh when Jerusalem will be assaulted by the nations, the city taken, and spoil divided among the attackers (cf. Zeph 1:7; Ezek 38–39). Houses will be plundered, women ravished (cf. Isa 13:16; Amos 7:17), and half of the city will go into exile. But then Yahweh will appear, standing on the Mount of Olives, and will fight against those nations. The Mount will be rent in two, probably by an earthquake (cf. Nah 1:5), and a remnant will escape to the great valley created between the divided mountain, extending all the way to Azel. Azel is an unknown destination. A comparison is made to the flight when an earthquake occurred during the reign of Uzziah, king of Judah (cf. Amos 1:1). With Yahweh will come all his holy ones, i.e., his angels (cf. Deut 33:2–3; Job 5:1; 15:15; Ps 89:5, 7 [Heb. 89:6, 8]; Dan 4:13; 8:13).

The Messianic Age commences (Driver). 14:6 is a difficult verse. What is clear is that day and night will be no more (Isa 60:20; Rev 22:5), maybe also cold and frost. In that day a perennial stream of water will go out from Jerusalem, half to the eastern sea, i.e., the Dead Sea, and half to the western sea, i.e., the Mediterranean, and it will irrigate

A Day of Yahweh is Coming (14:1–21)

the whole land (Ezek 47; Joel 3:18 [Heb. 4:18]; Rev 22:1–2). Yahweh will then be King over all the earth and will be worshiped by everyone as the one God having one name. Other gods go by different names; Yahweh has but one.

Judah will then sink and become like the Arabah, i.e., the Jordan Rift Valley through which the Jordan River flows, from Geba to Rimmon. Geba (modern Jaba') is ca. six miles northeast of Jerusalem (1 Sam 13:3, 16; 14:5; 1 Kgs 15:22; 2 Kgs 23:8: "from Geba to Beersheba"); Rimmon is nine miles north of Beersheba and about thirty-five miles southwest of Jerusalem ("En-rimmon" in Neh 11:29; "Ain and Rimmon" in Josh 15:32; and "Ain, Rimmon" in Josh 19:7; 1 Chr 4:32). Jerusalem, however, will remain in its place (12:1–6), prominently on high ground (Isa 2:2–3), with all her gates in place. The Gate of Benjamin was in the north wall of Jerusalem leading to the territory of Benjamin. It is the gate through which Jeremiah sought to leave the city to take care of business in Anathoth, but he was arrested and accused of deserting to the Babylonians (Jer 37:12–13). The First Gate, i.e., the Corner Gate, was a corner gate on the northwest corner of Jerusalem, about seven hundred feet to the west of the Gate of Ephraim (2 Kgs 14:13; Jer 31:38). They Tower of Hananel was in or near the northeast corner of Jerusalem, not far from the Benjamin Gate (Jer 31:38; Neh 3:1; 12:39). The king's wine vats were probably in or near the king's garden and the pool of Shelah (Neh 3:15), at the southeast corner of the city, not far from the former royal palace. Compare Jeremiah's promise of a rebuilt Jerusalem in Jer 31:38. Inhabitants of Jerusalem will dwell in security and no longer go into exile. The ban (Heb. *ḥerem*), derives from holy war, referring to captured spoil or inhabitants to be killed and devoted as a gift to Yahweh (Deut 7:2; 20:16–17; Josh 6:18–21; 1 Sam 15:3, 8; 1 Kgs 20:42). It will be no more.

II. ZECHARIAH

In this future day Yahweh will destroy the nations that have been warring against Jerusalem. A plague will fall upon both humans and beasts. The flesh of inhabitants will rot while they stand, their eyes will rot in their sockets, and their tongues will rot in their mouths. A great panic will seize them, causing one to slay another in the confusion. Even Judah will fight against Jerusalem. But Jerusalem will gain immense wealth from the nations.

Those surviving Yahweh's onslaught against the nations will become worshipers of the King and will keep the yearly Feast of Booths in Jerusalem (Deut 16:13–15). Drought will be the punishment for any not making the pilgrimage (cf. Amos 4:7). If Egypt does not go up, a plague will descend upon it.

Yahweh's crowning act will be to establish the holiness of Jerusalem (cf. Isa 4:3; Jer 31:40; Joel 3:17 [Heb. 4:17]). Even horses (foreigners riding in on pilgrimage?) will have bells upon them, for they too will be "holy to Yahweh." Every ordinary pot in the sanctuary will be as holy as bowls used to collect sacrificial blood; indeed, every pot in Judah and Jerusalem will be holy to Yahweh. And no Canaanite trader will enter the house of Yahweh in those days (Zeph 1:11; Joel 3:17 [Heb. 4:17]).

REFLECTION

1. In this passage Gentiles will join Jews in the worship of the Lord God. Can you find other such passages in Isaiah 40–66 or elsewhere in the OT?

2. Do you see a possible connection between the concluding words of 14:21 and Jesus' act of cleansing the Temple of traders in Matt 21:12–13 and John 2:13–22?

MALACHI

34

ISRAEL UNMINDFUL OF YAHWEH'S LOVE (1:2-5)

1 ¹An oracle. The word of Yahweh to Israel by Malachi.[1]
²I have loved you, said Yahweh. But you say, "How have you loved us?" Is not Esau Jacob's brother? oracle of Yahweh. Yet Jacob I have loved ³but Esau I have hated. I have made his hill country a desolation and his heritage a desert for jackals. ⁴If Edom says, "We are beaten down, but we will return and rebuild the ruins." Thus said Yahweh of hosts: They will build, but I will tear down, and they will be called the territory of wickedness, the people against whom Yahweh is angry forever. ⁵And your own eyes shall see and you shall say, "Great is Yahweh beyond the border of Israel!"

---

1. Or "my messenger."

RHETORIC AND COMPOSITION

THE PRESENT PASSAGE IS delimited largely on the basis of content; no section exists after 1:5 in the Hebrew Bible. It is generally agreed that the discourse of Malachi is prose, although the *BHS*, the *BHQ*, and Petersen scan some as poetry. Driver: 297–98 says:

> The style of Malachi is more prosaic than that of the prophets generally, though his sentences often fall into the rhythmical parallelism which is such a constant feature in the more elevated oratory of the prophets . . . He adopts also a novel literary form: first he states briefly the truth which he desires to enforce, then follows the objection which it is supposed to provoke, finally there comes the prophet's reply, reasserting and substantiating his original proposition (i. 2f., 6, 7, ii. 13f., 17, iii. 7, 8, 13). Thus in place of the rhetorical development of a subject, usual with the earlier prophets, there appears in Malachi a dialectical treatment by means of question and answer.

MESSAGE

Some people in Malachi's audience are questioning Yahweh's love for Israel, on which see Deut 7:7–8. Yahweh responds with another question, "Is not Esau Jacob's brother . . . Yet Jacob I have loved but Esau I have hated (cf. Rom 9:13). Reference is to Yahweh's choice of Jacob over Esau when Jacob (by deceit) was allowed to receive his father's blessing (Gen 27). The sharp "love-hate" contrast is due to a lack of relative particles in Hebrew. We see it also in Jacob's feelings toward Rachel and Leah (Gen 29:30–31). Nevertheless, here the words may mean exactly what they say, for Yahweh is reflecting Israel's inveterate hatred of Edom after the latter's complicity in the destruction of Jerusalem (Obad 8–14; Ezek 25:12; 35:5; Joel 3:19 [Heb. 4:19]; Ps 137:7). Yahweh is also stating here the theme of the whole book, viz., that his love for Israel is uncompromising (Smith).

Malachi is referring to some recent devastation of Edom, perhaps by the Nabataean Arabs (Driver), although one that may not have been permanent, since Edom is intending to rebuild. The exact date of the invasion is not known, nor also the date when the Edomite state came to an end. What we do know is that by 312 the Edomites had been permanently expelled from their homeland by the Nabataeans who came to occupy Mount Seir and the territory of Petra (Diodorus Siculus xix 94–100 cf. Bewer 1911:7). The Edomites were forced to move further in a westward direction into southern Judah (they had already entered southern Judah after the fall of Jerusalem), which came to be called Idumaea (cf. Mark 3:8). By the time of John Hyrcanus (134–103) Idumea had been incorporated into the Jewish commonwealth (Josephus *Ant* xiii 257). Yahweh says here that Edom's destruction will be permanent, causing people to say, "Great is Yahweh beyond the border of Israel!"

REFLECTION

1. Jacob and Esau had a rivalry throughout life, but in the last years were reconciled (Gen 33). Why do you think their descendants ended up hating one another? Does such thing happen in our own day?

35

IS YAHWEH PLEASED WITH POLLUTED ALTAR FOOD? (1:6—2:9)

⁶A son honors the father and a servant his master. If then I am a father, where is my honor? And if I am master, where is my respect? Yahweh of hosts has said to you, O priests, who despise my name. And you say, "How have we despised your name?" ⁷By offering polluted food on my altar. And you say, "How have we polluted you?" In saying "Yahweh's table is despised," ⁸and when you offer the blind for sacrifice: "It is no harm," and when you offer the lame or sick: "It is no harm." Present this to your governor! Will he be pleased with you or show you favor? said Yahweh of hosts. ⁹And now implore the favor of God that he may be gracious to us. From your hand this has come. Will he show favor to any of you? said Yahweh of hosts. ¹⁰Who is there

Is Yahweh Pleased with Polluted Altar Food? (1:6—2:9)

among you that could shut the Temple doors so you do not kindle fire on my altar in vain! I have no delight in you, said Yahweh of hosts, and I will not accept an offering from your hand. [11]For from the rising of the sun to its setting, great is my name among the nations. Yes, in every place incense is being offered in my name, and a [pure] offering, for great is my name among the nations, said Yahweh of hosts. [12]But you profane it when you say the Lord's table is polluted, and its fruit, its food, is despised. [13]And you say, "Look, what weariness!" And you sniff at it, said Yahweh of hosts. "And you bring what has been stolen, or lame, or sick, and you bring the offering! Shall I accept it from your hand?" said Yahweh. [14]Cursed be the cheat who has a male in his flock and he vows, yet he sacrifices one blemished to the Lord. For I am a great King, said Yahweh of hosts, and my name is revered among the nations.

2 [1]And now this command is to you, O priests. [2]"If you will not listen, and if you will not lay it to heart to give glory to my name," said Yahweh of hosts, "then I will send the curse against you and I will curse your blessings. Yes, I have already cursed it because you do not lay it to heart. [3]Look, I will rebuke your seed, and I will spread dung on your faces, the dung of your feasts, and he will carry you away to it. [4]And you shall know that I have sent this command to you, that my covenant might be with Levi, said Yahweh of hosts. [5]My covenant with him was one of life and peace, and I gave it to him to fear and he feared me and stood in awe of my name. [6]True instruction was in his mouth, and no wrong was found on his lips. In peace and uprightness he walked with me, and many he turned from iniquity. [7]For the lips of a priest should guard knowledge, and

instruction they should seek from his mouth, for he is the messenger of Yahweh of hosts. [8]But you have turned aside from the way; you have caused many to stumble by instruction; you have corrupted the covenant of Levi, said Yahweh of hosts. [9]So I also will make you despised and abased before all the people, inasmuch as you have not kept my ways and have shown partiality in instruction.

RHETORIC AND COMPOSITION

THIS NEXT PASSAGE IS delimited largely by theme, i.e., being about priests and altar worship. A sections also exists in the Hebrew Bible after 2:9. The Hebrew Bible has another section after 1:13, probably because of the concluding "said Yahweh."

The prophet continues in 1:6–14 with questions and answers, then in 2:1–9 levels a curse upon priests for deviating from Yahweh's covenant with Levi. One must be aware of the elliptical quality in much of this prophet's discourse. For example, in 1:11 where "offering" is the same Hebrew word (*minḥāh*) used in 1:10, meaning in 1:11 "pure offering." And in 1:12 the prophet says of his opponents, "But you profane it when *you say* the Lord's table is polluted, and its fruit, its food, is despised." They are not literally saying this; they are saying it by their actions.

MESSAGE

This prophecy begins by Yahweh pointing out that since a son honors his father (cf. Exod 20:12; Deut 5:16), and a servant his master, why then with Yahweh being a father and master to priests is their honor and respect not given

Is Yahweh Pleased with Polluted Altar Food? (1:6—2:9)

him? Priests are despising his name! How so? By offering polluted food on his altar. The priests want to know how they have polluted. They have treated Yahweh's table as despicable by offering blind, lame, and sick animals for sacrifices, saying, "It does no harm." The table is Yahweh's altar (Ezek 41:22; 44:16). Well, Yahweh says, try presenting gifts of this sort to the Persian governor. Will he be pleased and show you favor? The prophet then ironically suggests the priests implore God's favor so he may be gracious. Will he? Yahweh says he would rather someone shut the double doors leading to the Temple's inner court (Ezek 41:23-24) so priests could not kindle fire on his altar—for nothing! Yahweh has no delight in such priests and will not accept their offerings (Amos 5:21–22; Hos 8:13; Isa 1:11–13a). His name is great among the nations (cf. 1:5, 11). Other nations hold Yahweh's name in higher regard than do Israel's priests! (cf. Acts 10:35). Yahweh repeats his repudiation of polluted offerings that Levitical law forbids (Lev 1:3, 10; 3:1, 6; 4:3, 32; 22:20–24; etc.; cf. Deut 17:1). The priests respond by saying sanctuary service is a burden, and they sniff at it. The expression "And you sniff at it" is thought to originally have been "And you sniff at *me*," being one of 18 *Tiq soph* to avoid an offense to Yahweh (Zipor 1994). This first portion of the present prophecy closes with a curse on any "cheat" who vows to sacrifice a (pure) male animal from his flock and then, when paying the vow, sacrifices a blemished animal, another violation of Levitical law (Lev 22:18–24). Yahweh is a great King whose name is revered among the nations (cf. 1:5, 11).

Yahweh follows with an emphatic command to the priests. If the priests will not hear this rebuke and give glory to his name, then he will send a curse against them and make their blessings into curses. He has, in fact, already cursed them because they do not lay proper sacrifice to heart. What Yahweh will do is to prevent offspring from springing up, to spread dung removed from sacrificial animals on the faces of the priests, and to carry them away to where dung is thrown away (Driver; cf. Exod 29:14; Lev 4:11–12; 16:27). This is a brutal word to priests who abstain from anything unclean! Smith says this will be removal from Yahweh's presence, i.e., exile from the holy city and the Temple. The priests will be made to know Yahweh's command in order that his covenant with Levi might remain (Jer 33:21b), which was a covenant of life and peace (given through Phinehas; Num 25:10–13). Yahweh gave Levi the covenant of life and peace so priests would fear him, and Levi did fear and stand in awe of his name (cf. Deut 33:8–11). True instruction was in Levi's mouth, and no wrong came from his lips. Priests give oral instruction (cf. Jer 18:18). Levi walked with Yahweh in peace and uprightness, turning many from wrongdoing. "Walking with Yahweh" means intimate fellowship with Yahweh (Enoch in Gen 5:22, 24; Noah in Gen 6:9). Levi, like Isaiah, Jeremiah, and other prophets, was Yahweh's messenger (Hag 1:13; Eccl 5:6). Current priests, because of their turning aside from the proper way, have caused others to stumble, and in so doing have corrupted the covenant with Levi. Yahweh for his part will make them despised and abased before all the people since they did not keep his ways and have shown partiality in their instruction. Priests were also open to bribery (cf. Mic 3:11; Jer 6:13; 8:10).

REFLECTION

1. Do people today put "tainted money" in the offering plate or erect church and Christian schools with the same? Fund raisers are usually glad to get money regardless of the source. Does God care?

Is Yahweh Pleased with Polluted Altar Food? (1:6—2:9)

2. When we vow to the Lord are we quick to pay when our prayer has been answered?
3. Does your priest or pastor "walk with the Lord?" If not, he or she will cause others to stumble.

36

YAHWEH HATES DIVORCE! (2:10-16)

2 ¹⁰Have we not all one Father? Has not one God created us? Why then do we deal faithlessly each one to another, profaning the covenant of our fathers? ¹¹Judah has been faithless; yes, an abomination has been committed in Israel and in Jerusalem, for Judah has profaned the sanctuary of Yahweh that he loves and has married the daughter of a foreign god. ¹²May Yahweh cut off anyone who does this—caller or answerer—from the tents of Jacob and from bringing an offering to Yahweh of hosts.

¹³And this second thing you do: Cover with tears the altar of Yahweh, weeping and groaning, because he no longer regards the offering or accepts it with favor from your hand. ¹⁴And you say, "For what reason?" Because Yahweh is witness between you and the wife of your youth, to whom you have been faithless, though she is

your companion and the wife of your covenant. ¹⁵And did he not make [us] one? And a remnant of spirit is his. And what does the One seek? Godly offspring. So take heed with your spirit, and to the wife of your youth; let him not be faithless. ¹⁶For he[1] hates divorce, said Yahweh the God of Israel, also one who covers his garment with violence, said Yahweh of hosts. So take heed with your spirit and do not be faithless.

RHETORIC AND COMPOSITION

THE HEBREW BIBLE CONCLUDES the passage with a section after 2:16, but the chapter division occurs after 2:17. Driver places 2:17 with what follows, noting that its final question, "Where is the God of justice?" is answered in 3:1–6. A section in the Hebrew Bible appears after the concluding "Yahweh of hosts" in 2:12, perhaps because 2:13 begins, "And this second thing you do." Perhaps two oracles have been combined, the first dealing with profaning Yahweh's sanctuary when men marry "the daughter of a foreign god" (2:10–12), and the second dealing with men divorcing wives of their youth to marry foreign women (2:13–16).

MESSAGE

This passage shifts from priests to ordinary Judahite men who are unfaithful to wives of their youth by divorcing them to marry foreign women. This has resulted in Yahweh's not accepting their offerings at his altar. The problem is dealt with in Ezra 9–10 and Neh 13:23–29. God is a Father to

---

1. Reading of the Hebrew. Commentators following the Versions usually change to "I" because of the following "said Yahweh God of Israel."

Israel (1:6; cf. Deut 32:6; Isa 63:16). The prophet then asks, why the widespread faithlessness to the covenant of their fathers? The expression "covenant of your fathers" appears in Deut 4:31. The covenant not to marry the "daughter of a foreign god" (Exod 34:16; Deut 7:3–4) could be the covenant made at Sinai (Hill; cf. Exod 19:5–6) or the covenant of a perpetual priesthood given to Phinehas (Num 25:10–13; cf. Neh 13:28–29). On being faithful to one's wife, see Prov 5:15–23. All Judah has been faithless to Yahweh (cf. Jer 3:20), an abomination when men marry daughters of a foreign god and profane the sanctuary Yahweh loves. "Abomination" (Heb. *tô'ēbâh*) is a strong word (cf. Deut 13:14 [Heb. 13:15]; Ezra 9:14). May Yahweh cut off any man, one who calls or one who answers, from the worshiping community and from bringing an offering to Yahweh. "Caller or answerer" is said to be a proverbial expression meaning "everyone" (cf. "bond or free" in 1 Kgs 21:21), perhaps derived from watchmen making their nightly rounds (Driver, following Gesenius).

The prophet returns to the subject of divorce. Men are covering Yahweh's altars with tears, weeping and groaning, because Yahweh no longer accepts their offerings. They want to know why. The prophet has already told them: Because they have been faithless to the wife of their youth (cf. Prov 2:17). 2:15 is a difficult verse. The prophet appears to be saying that the One [God; cf. 2:10] is concerned about godly offspring. So take heed! Yahweh hates divorce! Yahweh also hates he who covers his garments with violence, i.e., ill-treats his wife. The practice of a man spreading his garment over a woman symbolizes his choice of her for a wife (Ruth 3:9; Ezek 16:8). In conclusion the prophet admonishes individuals to pay heed to their [inner] spirit and be not faithless.

Jesus addresses the problem of men divorcing their wives *in order to* marry another woman, calling it adultery (Mark 10:11).

REFLECTION

1. Do you believe the Lord hates divorce? Do you believe that Jesus' teaching in Mark 10:2–12, especially vv 10–12, has to do with "third party involvement? Matthew has another view on divorce (Matt 5:32). What about Paul's teaching in 1 Cor 7:10–11?

2. Is it a good idea for someone to marry a person of another religion? How about a Christian marrying an unbeliever? Every pastor has had to deal with this.

37

YAHWEH'S MESSENGER TO PREPARE THE WAY (2:17—3:12)

2 ¹⁷You have wearied Yahweh with your words, yet you say, "How have we wearied?" When you say, "Everyone who does evil is good in the eyes of Yahweh, and he delights in them," or "Where is the God of justice?"

3 ¹See, I am sending my messenger and he shall prepare the way before me, and the Lord whom you seek will suddenly come to his Temple. And the messenger of the covenant in whom you delight—see, he is coming, said Yahweh of hosts. ²But who can endure the day of his coming, and who can stand when he appears? For he is like a refiner's fire and like fullers' soap; ³and he will sit as a refiner and purifier of silver and will purify the sons of Levi and refine them like gold and silver until they present offerings to Yahweh in righteousness. ⁴Then the offering of Judah and Jerusalem will be pleasing to Yahweh as in

Yahweh's Messenger to Prepare the Way (2:17—3:12)

the days of old and as in former years. ⁵Then I will draw near to you for judgment; I will be a swift witness against the sorcerers and against the adulterers, against those who swear falsely, against those who oppress the hired worker in his wages, the widow and the orphan, and against those who thrust aside the alien, and do not fear me, said Yahweh of hosts. ⁶For I Yahweh do not change; therefore you, O sons of Jacob, have not perished.

⁷From the days of your fathers you have turned aside from my statutes and have not kept them. Return to me, and I will return to you, said Yahweh of hosts. But you say, "How shall we return?" ⁸Will a man rob God? Yet you are robbing me! But you say, "How are we robbing you?" In your tithes and offerings! ⁹You are cursed with a curse, for you are robbing me—this whole nation! ¹⁰Bring the full tithe into the storehouse that there may be food in my house, and test me now in this, said Yahweh of hosts, if I will not open the windows of heaven and pour down for you a more than sufficient blessing. ¹¹And I will rebuke the locust for you, that it will not destroy the produce of your soil, and your vine in the field shall not be barren, said Yahweh of hosts. ¹²Then all nations will count you happy, for you will be a land of delight, said Yahweh of hosts.

RHETORIC AND COMPOSITION

THIS PASSAGE HAS A section before 2:17 in the Hebrew Bible and another section after 3:12. Envisioned in 2:17 and 3:7–8 are objections to the prophet's words like those appearing in 1:2, 6–7; and 2:3–4. Another occurs in 3:13.

Smith thinks the question-and-answer style comes at the opening of a new phase of discourse.

The passage begins and ends with the word "delight:"

> 2:17 "... and he [Yahweh] *delights* in them"
> 3:12 "for you will be a land of *delight*"

MESSAGE

The prophet begins by telling people that they have exhausted Yahweh's patience with their words (cf. Isa 43:24). How so? By saying that everyone who does evil is good in the eyes of Yahweh and that he delights in them, or by asking, "Where is the God of justice?" Faith in Yahweh is at a low ebb: both bad and good are said to delight Yahweh, and people are unable to see the hand of God in anything taking place.

Yahweh, however, comes with an answer to this malaise: He is sending his messenger to prepare the way before him, and a day of judgment it will be. The messenger is a prophet (Ross 1962) whose identity is not given. This coming one is mentioned again at the conclusion of Malachi's prophecy (4:5–6). On preparing the way for an oncoming king, see Isa 40:3. The present verse, or perhaps Isa 40:3, is cited by Jesus in Matt 11:10 and Luke 7:27 (also Mark 1:2), where it is said to have been fulfilled in John the Baptist.

Yahweh is going to come suddenly into his Temple. On the sudden in Scripture, see Daube 1964. But who can endure the day of his coming (cf. Amos 5:18–20; Zeph 1:14–18), for things in the Temple are in a deplorable state. Yahweh will come like a refiner's fire (cf. Jer 6:27–30; Zech 13:9) and fullers' soap (i.e., lye; Job 9:30), and he will purify the sons of Levi until they present their Temple offerings in righteousness. Then offerings will be pleasing to Yahweh as in days of old. Yahweh at this time will act decisively against sorcerers (cf. Exod 22:18 [Heb. 22:17]; Deut 18:10), adulterers, and perjurers (cf. Exod 20:16; Deut 5:20; 19:16–19; Lev 19:12; Zech 5:4), all of whom bear responsibility for community breakdown. In the days of Malachi, sorcerers were practitioners of magic, bewitching people and casting evil spells upon them (cf. Acts 8:9; 13:6). Hired workers were being oppressed, and people were acting unjustly to resident aliens, orphans, and widows, all forbidden in the Covenant and Deuteronomic Codes (Exod 22:21–22; Deut 24:14–15, 17). Yahweh's moral character remains unchanged, which is why Israel has not been utterly consumed (cf. Jer 30:11).

Yahweh says that from ancient times people have turned aside from his statutes. "Return to me," he says, "and I will return to you" (cf. Zech 1:3; Jer 4:1). People want to know how they have revolted. Yahweh, still the speaker, says they have been robbing him. How so? In the paying of tithes and offerings. They are to bring the full tithe into the storehouse so there may be food in Yahweh's house (cf. Neh 10:38; 12:44; 13:5, 12–13). Prophets in ancient Assyria censured kings for not supplying the gods with sacrificial food in the temples (Lundbom 2016: 9). Yahweh calls upon the people to test him and see if he will not open the windows of heaven and pour down a more than sufficient blessing of rain. Testing Yahweh was allowable under certain circumstances (Exod 4:1–9; Judg 6:36–40; Isa 7:10–17), but one must be careful about doing so (Deut 6:16; Matt 4:7). There had apparently been a drought. Yahweh promises to rebuke the locust, that terrible curse in antiquity, known also in modern times across the Near East and Africa (Joel 1:4; Lundbom 2023: 25–26), which in no time lays bare trees, field crops, and vineyards. The result of Yahweh's goodness will be that nations will count Judahites happy, for their land will be a land of delight (cf. Isa 62:4).

Three verses from this passage were used by G. F. Handel in his *Messiah* oratorio:

Messiah Part 1

Movement 1: Overture (symphony only)

Movement 5: Mal 3:1

> The Lord, whom ye seek, shall suddenly come to His temple, even the messenger of the covenant, whom you delight in: behold, He shall come, saith the Lord of hosts.

Movement 6: Mal 3:2

> But who may abide the day of His coming? and who shall stand when He appeareth? For He is like a refiner's fire.

Movement 7: Mal 3:3

> And He shall purify the sons of Levi, that they may offer unto the Lord an offering in righteousness.

REFLECTION

1. Do you ever feel as if God closes his eyes to evil and courts failing to exercise justice? Jeremiah did (Jer 12:1–4). What can you do at such a time?
2. Do you believe the Lord's words: "Return to me and I will return to you"?
3. How today do we bring the full tithe into the storehouse?
4. Are you careful about putting the Lord to the test?

38

A BOOK OF REMEMBRANCE (3:13-18)

3 ¹³You have spoken harsh words against me, said Yahweh. Yet you say, "How have we spoken against you?" ¹⁴You have said, "It is vain to serve God and what do we profit by keeping his command or walking about as mourners before Yahweh of hosts? ¹⁵Yes, now we count the arrogant happy; indeed, evildoers not only prosper but when they put God to the test they escape." ¹⁶Then they who revered Yahweh spoke with one another. Yahweh took note and listened, and a book of remembrance was written before him of those who revered Yahweh and thought on his name. ¹⁷They shall be mine, said Yahweh of hosts, in the day that I make a treasure piece, and I will spare them as a man spares his own son who serves him. ¹⁸Then you shall return and discern between the righteous

and the wicked, between one who serves God and one who does not serve him.

RHETORIC AND COMPOSITION

THERE ARE SECTIONS IN in the Hebrew Bible before 3:13 and after 3:18. The passage begins with another question and answer.

MESSAGE

Yahweh begins here by saying that people have spoken strong words against him. How have they done so? They have said it is of no profit to serve Yahweh, or they ask what profit there is to keep his command or walk before him in mourning apparel. Does the mourning garb indicate genuine repentance? Joel says, "Rend your heart and not your garments" (Joel 2:12–13a). According to Malachi, his people are calling the arrogant happy, for evildoers not only prosper but put God to the test and escape. The testing could be that called for in 3:10. Jeremiah asks Yahweh why the wicked prosper (Jer 12:1), and Habakkuk asks why Yahweh looks upon the treacherous and is silent when the wicked are swallowing up the righteous (Hab 1:13). But Ps 1 says Yahweh knows the way of the righteous, but the way of the wicked will perish (Ps 1:6).

Pious Judahites after hearing these words get together and speak with one another, and Yahweh listens. A book (i.e., a scroll or tablet) of remembrance is then written, with the names of those who revered Yahweh and regarded his name. Driver says:

> [It was] the custom of the Persian monarchs to have the names of public benefactors inscribed

A Book of Remembrance (3:13–18)

in a book in order that in due time they might receive a suitable reward.

See the "book of records" in Est 6:1–3 and compare written records in Isa 4:3; Ps 69:28 [Heb. 69:29]; and Rev 20:12. Similarly, Yahweh says that on the day he makes a treasure piece he will spare the pious as a man spares his own son. On all Israel being Yahweh's treasure piece, see Exod 19:5; Deut 7:6; 14:2; 26:18; Ps 135:4; cf. 1 Pet 2:9. At that time the rebellious community will return to Yahweh and be able to distinguish the righteous from the wicked, between one who serves God and one who does not.

REFLECTION

1. Do you ever feel that evildoers prosper?
2. Are arrogant people happy, really happy?

39

THE DAY IS COMING (4:1-3 [HEB. 3:19-21])

4 ¹For indeed the day is coming, burning like an oven, when all the arrogant and all evildoers will be stubble; yes, the day that comes shall burn them up, said Yahweh of hosts, so it will leave them neither root nor branch. ²But for you who revere my name the sun of righteousness will rise with healing in its wings. And you will go out leaping like calves from the stall. ³And you will tread down the wicked, for they will be ashes under the soles of your feet in the day when I act, said Yahweh of hosts.

RHETORIC AND COMPOSITION

4:1–3 CONTINUES AS 3:19–21 in the MT of the Hebrew Bible. The LXX, Vg, and some Hebrew MSS begin a new chapter at 3:19. The Hebrew Bible has sections before 3:19

The Day Is Coming (4:1–3 [Heb. 3:19–21])

and after 3:21. The present passage is linked to the prior one by "day" and "wicked" (3:17–18; 4:3). It is also held together by this key word inclusio:

4:1   For behold *the day* is coming

4:3   . . . in *the day* when I act

MESSAGE

Here is why the righteous and wicked in 3:18 are to be distinguished. On Yahweh's coming day, burning like an oven, the arrogant and all evildoers will burn like stubble, with nothing remaining—a reversal of the skeptics' judgment in 3:15. But for those who revere Yahweh's name a beaming sun of righteousness will rise with healing in its wings, leaving them leaping for joy at their release. On that day they will trample down the wicked, who will be ashes from Yahweh's fire. On the origin of the "Day of Yahweh," see von Rad 1959.

REFLECTION

1. Have you ever felt the sun rising in your life with healing in its wings? What happened?

40

I WILL SEND ELIJAH THE PROPHET (4:4-6 [HEB. 3:22-24])

4 ⁴Remember the teaching of my servant Moses that I commanded him at Horeb for all Israel, the statutes and ordinances. ⁵Behold, I will send you the prophet Elijah before the great and terrible day of Yahweh comes. ⁶And he will turn the heart of the fathers to the children and the heart of the children to their fathers, lest I come and strike the land with a curse.

RHETORIC AND COMPOSITION

THESE VERSES MAY BE a later addition to Malachi's book (Smith; Achtemeier).

I Will Send Elijah the Prophet (4:4–6 [Heb. 3:22–24])

MESSAGE

This concluding word of Malachi admonishes hearers to remember Moses's teachings at Horeb, but the "statutes and ordinances" are those Moses delivered later in the plains of Moab (Deut 11:1, 31). Yahweh now promises to send remnant Judahites the prophet Elijah, who was carried up into heaven at the conclusion of his ministry (2 Kgs 2:11). On the "great and terrible day of Yahweh," see Joel 2:31 [Heb. 3:4]. Elijah will restore unity to a divided community (cf. Mark 9:11–12; Matt 11:11–14; Luke 1:16–17), lest Yahweh come and strike the land with destruction (cf. Zech 14:11). Elijah is given a eulogy in the Apocryphal book of Sirach (48:1–11). In Jewish tradition, the prophecy of Malachi—indeed the entire prophetic corpus—could not end with a curse, so the penultimate verse was repeated in a public reading after the final verse was read. The same occurred when rabbis read the final verse of Isaiah (Isa 66:24).

In modern Jewish celebrations of Passover, at the conclusion of the Seder meal, a young child is sent to open the door of the room as a symbolic welcome to Elijah. For Christians, however, Elijah has already come in the person of John the Baptist (Matt 11:11–14; 17:10–13; Mark 9:11–13).

REFLECTION

1. How could John the Baptist be regarded as Elijah having returned? When Jesus returns might he be born and have another name?

2. Did John the Baptist turn the hearts of fathers and mothers to their children? Or did his coming divide some families? See Matt 11:16–19.

MALACHI

Answer to question about dealings with the Greeks: Ezekiel (Ezek 27:13, 19), III Isaiah (Isa 66:19), and Joel (Joel 3:6 [Heb. 4:6]).

BIBLIOGRAPHY

Achtemeier, Elizabeth. *Nahum–Malachi*. IBC. Atlanta: John Knox, 1986.
Aharoni, Yohanan. *Arad Inscriptions*. Translated by Judith Ben-Or. Edited and revised by Anson F. Jerusalem: Israel Exploration Society, 1981.
Albright, William F. *The Biblical Period from Abraham to Ezra*. Rev. ed. Harper Torchbooks. Cloister Library 102. New York: Harper & Row, 1963.
Berridge, John M. *Prophet, People, and the Word of Yahweh*. Zurich: EVZ, 1970).
Bewer, Julius. *A Critical and Exegetical Commentary on Obadiah and Joel*. ICC. Edinburgh: T. & T. Clark, 1911.
Boda, Mark J. *The Book of Zechariah*. NICOT. Grand Rapids: Eerdmans, 2016.
Bright, John. *A History of Israel*. 3rd ed. Westminster Aids to the Study of the Scriptures. Philadelphia: Westminster, 1981.
Cathcart, Kevin J., and Robert P. Gordon. *The Targum to the Minor Prophets*. ArBib 14. Wilmington, DE: Glazier, 1989.
Daube, David. *The Sudden in the Scriptures*. Leiden: Brill. 1964.
Driver, S. R. ed. *The Minor Prophets*. Vol. 2, *Nahum, Habakkuk, Zephaniah, Haggai, Zechariah, Malachi*. Century Bible. Edinburgh: Jack, 1906.
Ego, Beate, et al., eds. *Biblia Qumranica*. Vol. 3B, *Minor Prophets*. Leiden: Brill, 2005.
Eissfeldt, Otto. *The Old Testament: An Introduction*. Translated by Peter R. Ackroyd. New York: Harper & Row, 1965.
Freedman, David Noel, and Jack R. Lundbom. "*ḥānan* (to show favor, grace)." In *TDOT* 5:22–36. Reprinted in Lundbom, *Theology in*

Language, Rhetoric, and Beyond, 1–20. Eugene, OR: Cascade Books, 2014.

Gaster. Theodor H., trans. *The Dead Sea Scriptures*. Rev. 3rd ed. Garden City, NY: Anchor Press/Doubleday, 1976.

Heschel, Abraham Joshua. *The Prophets*. New York: Harper & Row, 1962.

Hill, Andrew E. "Malachi, Book of." In *ABD* 4:478–85.

———. *Malachi*. AB 25D. New York: Doubleday, 1998.

Josephus, Flavius. *Josephus VI: Jewish Antiquities: Books 9–11*. Translated by Ralph Marcus. LCL. Cambridge: Harvard University Press, 1967.

———. *Josephus VII: Jewish Antiquities: Books 12–14*. Translated by Ralph Marcus. LCL. Cambridge: Harvard University Press, 1966.

Köhler, Ludwig. "Appendix: Justice in the Gate." In *Hebrew Man*, 147–75. Translated by Peter R. Ackroyd. London: SCM, 1956.

Lundbom, Jack R. "Builders of Ancient Babylon: Nabopolassar and Nebuchadnezzar II." *Int* 71 (2017) 154–66.

———. *Deuteronomy: A Commentary*. Grand Rapids: Eerdmans, 2013.

———. "God's Use of the *Idem per Idem* to Terminate Debate." *HTR* 71 (1978) 193–201.

———. *The Hebrew Prophets: An Introduction*. Minneapolis: Fortress, 2010.

———. *Jeremiah 1–20*. AB 21A. New York: Doubleday / New Haven: Yale University Press, 1999.

———. *Jeremiah 21–36*. AB 21B. New York: Doubleday / New Haven: Yale University Press, 2004.

———. *Joel: Prophet of the Outpouring Spirit*. A Critical Commentary. Sheffield: Sheffield Phoenix, 2023.

Malamat, Abraham. "The Last Wars of the Kingdom of Judah." *JNES* 9 (1950) 218–27.

Meyers, Carol L., and Eric M. Meyers. *Haggai, Zechariah 1–8*. AB 25B. Garden City, NY: Doubleday, 1987.

Mitchell, Hinkley G. "Haggai and Zechariah." In *A Critical and Exegetical Commentary on Haggai, Zechariah, Malachi, and Jonah*, edited by Hinkley G. Mitchell et al., 3–357. ICC. 1912. Reprint, Edinburgh: T. & T. Clark, 1999.

Muilenburg, James. "Old Testament Prophecy." In *Peake's Commentary on the Bible*, edited by Mathew Black and H. H. Rowley, 475–83. 1962. Reprint, London: Nelson, 1977.

Petersen, David L. *Haggai and Zechariah 1–8: A Commentary*. OTL. Philadelphia: Westminster, 1984.

———, ed. *Prophecy in Israel: Search for an Identity*. Issues in Religion and Theology 10. Philadelphia: Fortress, 1987.

———. *Zechariah 9–14 and Malachi*. OTL. Louisville: Westminster John Knox, 1995.

Rad, Gerhard von. "The Origin of the Concept of the Day of Yahweh." *JSS* 4 (1959) 97–108.

Ross, James F. "The Prophet as Yahweh's Messenger." In *Israel's Prophetic Heritage: Essays in Honor of James Muilenburg*, edited by Bernhard W. Anderson and Walter Harrelson, 98–107. New York: Harper, 1962. Reprinted in David Petersen 1987: 112–21.

Smith, John Merlin Powis. *Malachi*. In *A Critical and Exegetical Commentary on Haggai, Zechariah, Malachi, and Jonah*, edited by Hinkley G. Mitchell et al., 3–85. ICC. 1912. Reprinted, Edinburgh: T. & T. Clark, 1999.

Tadmor, Hayim. "Chronology of the Last Kings of Judah." *VT* 15 (1956) 226–30.

Tristram, H. B. *The Natural History of the Bible*. 9th ed. 1867. Reprint, London: SPCK, 1898.

———. *The Survey of Western Palestine: The Fauna and Flora of Palestine*. London: Committee of the Palestine Exploration Fund, 1884.

Williamson, H. G. M. *Ezra–Nehemiah*. WBC 16. Grand Rapids: Zondervan, 1985.

Wolff, Hans Walter. *Haggai: A Commentary*. Translated by Margaret Kohl. CC. Minneapolis: Augsburg, 1988.

Xenophon. *Xenophon II: Cyropaedia; V–VIII*. Translated by Walter Miller. LCL. New York: Macmillan, 1914.

Zipor, Moshe A. "Some Notes on the Origin of the Tradition of the Eighteen TIQQÛNÊ SÔPERÎM." *VT* 44 (1994) 77–102.

NAME INDEX

Achtemeier, Elizabeth, 21, 41, 52, 92, 170
Aharoni, Yohanan, 2
Albright, William F., 5
Augustine, 9

Berridge, John M., 73
Bewer, Julius, 149
Boda, Mark J., 21, 23, 125, 129, 133, 134
Bright, John, 2–6, 8

Daube, David, 162
Driver, S. R., 46, 52, 66, 79, 83, 85, 129, 130, 134, 142, 148, 149, 154, 157, 158, 166

Ehrlich, A. B., 90
Eissfeldt, Otto, 9

Freedman, David Noel, 82

Gaster, Theodor H., 94
Gelston, Anthony, xii
Gesenius, William, 158

Handel, G. F., 52, 53, 120, 164

Heschel, Abraham, 10, 11, 12
Hill, Andrew E. 158

Kartveit, Magnar, xii
Kartveit, Marit, xii
Köhler, Ludwig, 103

Lundbom, Jack R., 3, 46, 67, 74, 82, 120, 163
Luther, Martin, 78, 79

MacArthur, Douglas, 8
Malamat, Abraham, 2
Meyers, Carol L., 67, 73, 79, 81, 82, 85, 87, 88
Meyers, Eric M., 67, 73, 79, 81, 82, 85, 87, 88
Mitchell, Hinkley G., 20, 21, 38, 52, 62, 66, 67, 73, 81, 83, 87, 88, 92, 115, 116

Petersen, David L., 21, 40, 46, 62, 65, 66, 67, 71, 73, 74, 77, 79, 81, 82, 83, 90, 92, 93, 94, 97, 100, 103, 105, 108, 120, 129, 133, 137, 141

Name Index

Rad, Gerhard von, 169
Rashi, 74
Ross, James F., 162

Smith, John Merlin Powis, 149, 162, 170

Tadmor, Hayim, 2

Tristram, H. B., 88

Williamson, H. G. M., 6
Wolff, Hans Walter, 13, 38, 40, 41, 46, 52

Zipor, Moshe, 153

SCRIPTURE INDEX

OLD TESTAMENT

Genesis

5:22	154
5:24	154
6:9	154
10:2	118
10:4	118
11:2	88
11:4	88
12:1–3	88
27	148
28:15	46
29:30–31	148
33	149
40:20	69
48:1	124
49:10–11	119

Exodus

3:12	46, 49
3:14	46
4:1–9	163
4:16	133
6:7	74
14:21–22	125
19:5–6	158
19:5	167
20:5	67
20:12	152
20:15–16	85
20:15	85
20:16	85, 103, 163
21:32	130
22:17 [Heb.]	163
22:18	163
22:21–22	163
23:7	103
24:1–8	119
24:6–8	120
25:31–40	82
28:9–21	79
28:36–38	79
29:14	154
33:14	49
34:16	158

Leviticus

1:3	153
1:5	120
1:10	153

Leviticus (continued)

1:11	120
3:1	153
3:6	153
4:3	15:3
4:11–12	154
4:32	153
6:27	56
10:10–11	55
16:27	154
17:10–14	115
17:10–11	116
19:12	163
22:18–24	153
22:20–24	153
26:12	74

Numbers

3:18	134
3:21	134
11:7	87
19:11–22	56
25:10–13	154, 158

Deuteronomy

3:8–20	125
4:24	67
4:31	158
5:9	67
5:16	152
5:19–20	85
5:19	85
5:20	85, 103, 163
6:4–5	106
6:16	163
7:2	143
7:3–4	158
7:6	167
7:7–8	148
7:13	43
10:8	134
11:1	171
11:12	79
11:14	43
11:24	119
11:31	171
12:16	115
12:17	43
12:23–24	115
12:23	116
13:1–10	137
13:2–11 [Heb.]	137
13:14	158
13:15 [Heb.]	158
14:2	167
14:3–21	115
16:11	106
16:13–15	144
16:14	106
17:1	153
18:10	163
18:14–15	12
19:16–19	103, 163
20:16–17	143
21:18–21	137
24:14–15	163
24:17	163
25:7	103
26:15	75
26:18	167
28:15–68	62
28:23	43
29:11–12 [Heb.]	74
29:12–13	74
32:6	158
32:10	74
33:2–3	142
33:8–11	154
33:17	69
34:14	67

Scripture Index

Joshua

1:4	119
1:5	46
6:18–21	143
15:32	143
19:7	143

Judges

5:16	124, 130
6:16	46
6:36–40	163
7:11	100
8:3	90
8:28	69
10:4	119
12:14	119
20:2	124

Ruth

3:9	158
4:1	103
4:11	103

1 Samuel

13:3	143
13:16	1
13:31–34	115
14:5	143
14:38	124
15:3	143
15:8	143
17:40	130

2 Samuel

5:6–9	116
5:14	134
5:17–25	116
7:1–3	41
7:2	41
8:1	116
8:3–8	116
10:15–19	116
14:17	133–134
16:2	119

1 Kings

4:21	116
4:25	79
5:1 [Heb.]	116
5:5 [Heb.]	79
6:9	41
7:3	41
7:49	82
8:16	58
8:44	67, 78
8:48	67
9:20	116
9:28	52
10:14–22	52
10:27	52
11:13	78
11:34	58
15:22	143
19:13	137
19:19	137
20:42	143
21:21	158
22:11	69

2 Kings

1:8	79, 137
2:8	137
2:11	171
2:13	137
14:13	143
14:25	116
17:5–41	38
23:8	143
23:29–30	134

2 Kings (continued)

24	1
24:10–15	38
24:16	2
24:20	2
25:1	106
25:3–5	106

1 Chronicles

3:16–17	38
3:17–19	5
3:18	4
4:32	143
5:34–41 [Heb.]	5
5:41 [Heb.]	38
6:8–15	5
6:15	38
21:1	77
25:4	66
25:8–9	49
25:18–21	38, 78
25:27–30	3
28:20	49

2 Chronicles

6:6	67
6:34	67
6:38	67
16:9	83
30:27	75
35:22–25	134
36:6	1
36:21	67
36:22–23	4

Ezra

1:1–4	4
1:7–11	4
2	13
2:2	38
3:2	5, 38
3:8	5
4:1–5	38, 39
4:1–3	94
4:1	100
4:6	6
5:1–2	6, 14
5:1	13, 38, 62
5:2	46
5:16	5
6:1–5	4
6:3–7	43
6:3	38
6:11	85
6:13–18	6
6:14	13, 14, 38, 62
6:15	52
7:1–8:36	6
7:1	38
7:8–9	6
9–10	157
9:14	158
10:4	49

Nehemiah

2:1–8	6
2:8	43
3:1	143
3:15	143
4:1–2	7
5:14	6, 7
5:14–18	26
6:15	7, 38
7	13
7:4	5
8	6
8:15–16	43
9:29	103
10:1	6

10:38	163	31:23	106
11:29	143	31:24 [Heb.]	106
12:1	38	33:16	119
12:4	14	34:15	79
12:16	62	34:16 [Heb.]	79
12:39	143	51:8	106
12:44	163	51:10 [Heb.]	106
13:4–9	7	66:7	79
13:5	163	69:28	167
13:12–13	163	69:29 [Heb.]	167
13:23–29	157	72:8	119
13:28–29	158	89:5	142
		89:6 [Heb.]	142
		89:7	142
		89:8 [Heb.]	142

Esther

6:1–3	167

Job

1:6–12	77
1:7	66
2:1–8b	77
2:2	66
5:1	142
5:4	103
9:30	162
15:15	142
29:14	78
39:19–25	124

Psalms

1	166
1:6	166
11:4	79
15:2	103
17:8	74
18:42	124
18:43 [Heb.]	124
22:12	69
22:13 [Heb.]	69
26:8	75

104:4	90
104:15	124
107:24	66
135:4	167
137	62
137:7	2, 149
138	62
145	62
146	62
147	62
148	62

Proverbs

2:17	158
5:15–23	158
6:16–19	103
30:12	78

Ecclesiastes

5:6	154
7:8	83
10:4	90
10:19	124

Isaiah

Reference	Page
1:11–13a	153
1:26	97
2:2–3	108, 143
2:4	119
4:3	144, 167
4:4	78
5:8	73
5:11	73
5:18	73
5:20	73
5:21–22	73
5:26	125
6:3	73
6:8	46
6:10	103
7:10–17	163
7:14	108
7:18	125
8:3–4	79
8:17	67
8:18	79
9:3 [Heb.]	125
9:4	125
9:5 [Heb.]	119
9:6	119
10:12–14	125
10:32	74
11:3–5	119
11:11	88
11:15	74, 125
13:16	142
14:9	124
14:24–27	12
16:6	119
19:13	124
19:16–25	7
19:16	74
20	115
22:13	106
26:8	67
29:21	103
30:18	67
31:4–5	133
32:1	119
33:12	67
35:3	100
35:10	106
40–66	144
40:1	67
40:2	120
40:3	162
41:1–7	3
41:10	46
41:25	73
43:2	125
43:5–6	98
43:5	46
43:24	162
45:9	73
45:14	52, 74, 94
45:14b	108
45:16	94
46:1–2	3
47:5–7	67
48:20	73
49:5–6	10
49:19–20	71
49:20	125
51:3	106
51:11	106
52:16b	73
54:1–3	125
54:2–3	71
55:1	73
55:5	74, 94, 108
56:2b	11
56:3–8	94, 108
56:3–7	74
56:11–12	130
60:1–2	71
60:3	74, 94, 108

Scripture Index

60:4–7	94	7:5	62
60:5	52	7:13	103
60:10	94	7:24	62
60:11	52, 94	7:26–27	103
60:13	49, 52	7:34	106
60:16	52, 94	8:7	88
60:17–18	52	8:10	154
60:19	71	9:22–23 [Heb.]	11
60:20	142	9:23–24	11
61:4	49	10:20	133
61:5–6	94	10:22	73
61:6	52	11:10	103
62:4	164	12:1–4	164
63:16	158	12:1	166
65:20	97	12:7	116
65:25	33	13:11	103
66:12	94	14:14	12
66:24	171	15:16	106
		15:20	46

Jeremiah

		16:9	106
1:5	12	16:18	120
1:7	46	17:1	103
1:8	46	17:10	62
1:11–14	66	17:18	120
1:14	73	18:11	62
1:19	46	18:18	154
2:18	119	21:5	103
3:12–15	62	22:4	119
3:12	119	22:13	73
3:18	73, 119	22:14	41
3:20	158	22:18–19	1
4:1	163	22:24	58, 93
4:20	133	23:5–6	5
6:10	103	23:5	78, 93, 119
6:13	154	23:8	73
6:16–17	103	23:22	62
6:19	103	23:28–32	12
6:22	73	25:4–5	62
6:26	134	25:5	62
6:27–30	162	25:10	106
7:3	62	25:11–12	4

Jeremiah (continued)

25:11	67
25:20	115
25:30	75
25:34–38	124
26:3	62
26:12–14	10
26:13	62
27–28	2
27:9–10	12
27:9	12
28:8	12
29:1–2	1
29:2	8
29:6	125
29:8–9	2
29:8	12
29:10	4, 67
29:19	62
29:21–23	2
30:4	46
30:10–11	97
30:11	163
30:18	133
30:22	74, 98
31:1–20	125
31:1	74, 98
31:2–9	119
31:6	119
31:9	119
31:12	43
31:15–20	119
31:18	119
31:20	119
31:23	97
31:28	103
31:33	98
31:38–40	67
31:38	143
31:40	144
33:11	106
33:13	106
33:14–15	6
33:15	78, 93, 119
33:21b	154
35:15	62
35:16–17	62
35:17	103
37:12–13	143
39:3	3
39:13	3
39:36	73
43:8–13	3
46:27–28	98
48:25	69
49:29	133
49:36	90
50:8	73
50:9	73
51:6	73
51:45	73
51:59	2
52:3	2
52:6–8	106
52:12–13	49
52:19	82
52:24–27	38, 78
52:28	2
52:29	2
52:30	3
52:31	69

Lamentations

2:20	14, 97

Ezekiel

3:9	103
3:23	73
5:13	90
6:7	74
6:10	74

6:13	74	4:13	142
6:14	74	8:13	142
11:3	38		
11:19	103	**Hosea**	
13:1–9	12		
16:8	158	2:17	137
23:6	124	2:18	130
23:12	124	2:19 [Heb.]	137
23:23	124	2:20 [Heb.]	130
25:12	2, 149	4:6	103
27:13	172	4:17	119, 124
27:19	172	5:3	119, 124
28:3–4	115	5:5	119, 124
33:25	115	5:9	119
34:1–6	130	8:13	153
34:16	130	9:15	116
34:17	124	14:2–4	62
34:25	130		
35:5	2, 149	**Joel**	
36:5–6	97		
36:17	137	1:4	163
36:25	137	2:12–13a	166
37:9	90	2:31	171
37:15–28	125	3:4 [Heb.]	171
37:23	137	3:6	172
38–39	142	3:17	97, 144
38:15	73, 124	3:18	143
39:2	73	3:19	2, 149
40–48	49	4:6 [Heb.]	172
41:22	153	4:17 [Heb.]	97, 144
41:23–24	153	4:18 [Heb.]	143
43:1–2	71	4:19 [Heb.]	2, 149
43:4–5	71		
44:15	78	**Amos**	
44:16	153		
47	143	1:1	66, 142
48:11	78	1:3—2:6	12
		1:6–8	115
		4:6–12	62
Daniel		4:7	144
		4:9	56
2:5	85	4:11	78
3:29	85		

Amos (continued)

5:15	103, 106
5:18–20	162
5:21–22	153
6:1	73
7:1–9	65–66
7:17	142
8:1–3	66
9:3	43

Obadiah

8–14	2, 149
17	97
20	125

Micah

3:11	154
4:1–2	74, 94, 108
4:3	119
4:4	79
4:13	69
5:9 [Heb.]	119
5:10	119
6:7	134
7:10	124

Nahum

1:2	67
1:5	142
3:18	124

Habakkuk

1:13	166
2:3	67
2:20	75
3:7	133
3:13b	85

Zephaniah

1:7	75, 142
1:11	144
1:14–18	162
3:8	67
3:14–15	74, 119
3:17b–18a	106

Haggai

1:1–2	13, 37–39
1:1	5, 37, 46, 114
1:2	37, 100
1:3–6	13, 40–41
1:3	40
1:4–6	40
1:4	40, 41
1:5	40, 41, 43
1:6	13, 40, 41, 56, 100
1:7–11	13, 42–44
1:7	41, 42, 43
1:8	42
1:9	42
1:10–11	13, 100
1:10	42
1:11	42, 43
1:12–15	13, 45–47
1:12–14	46
1:12	5, 45, 97
1:13	10, 45, 66, 154
1:14–15	55
1:14	5, 45, 49, 97
1:15	45, 46
2	46
2:1–5	14, 48–50, 56, 62
2:1	48, 49
2:2	48, 97

Scripture Index

2:3–5	49	1:1	14, 22, 61, 134
2:3	48, 82		
2:4	46, 48, 100	1:2	61, 62, 67, 103
2:5	48–49, 49, 82	1:3	61, 163
2:6–9	14, 51–53, 56, 62	1:3b	62
		1:4	61, 103
2:6–7	52, 66	1:4b–6	62
2:6	51, 52	1:5–6	62
2:7	51, 52, 94	1:5	61
2:8	51	1:6	61, 62
2:9	51, 52	1:7—6:8	14
2:10–19	14, 54–56	1:7–17	15, 17, 64–67, 90
2:10	54		
2:11	54	1:7	14, 64
2:12	54	1:8	64, 90
2:13	54	1:9	64
2:14–18a	55	1:10–11	90
2:14	54	1:10	64
2:15–19	46	1:11	64–65
2:15–17	41	1:12	65
2:15	55	1:13	65
2:16–17	100	1:14–17	13
2:16	13, 55	1:14–15	124
2:17	55	1:14	65
2:18–23	66	1:14b–17	65
2:18	55	1:14b	97
2:19	13, 55, 100	1:15	65, 90, 97
2:20–23	5, 14, 57–58	1:16	65, 71
2:20–22	66	1:16b	97
2:20	57, 58	1:17	65, 75, 78
2:21	57	1:18–21	15, 68–69
2:21b–22	58	1:18	68
2:22	57	1:19	68
2:23	57, 79, 93	1:20	68
		1:21	66, 68
		2:1–5	15, 70–71
		2:1–4 [Heb.]	15, 68–69
		2:1	70
		2:1 [Heb.]	68, 70
		2	11

Zechariah

1–14	20, 21
1–8	14, 20, 21
1:1–6	14, 15, 56, 61–63, 66

Zechariah (continued)

2:2	70
2:2 [Heb.]	68
2:3	66, 70
2:3 [Heb.]	68
2:4	70
2:4 [Heb.]	68
2:5–9 [Heb.]	15, 70–71
2:5	70, 73, 74
2:5 [Heb.]	70
2:6–13	15, 72–75
2:6–12	13
2:6–7	90
2:6	69, 72, 90
2:6 [Heb.]	70
2:7	72, 73
2:7 [Heb.]	70
2:8	10, 72
2:8 [Heb.]	70
2:8b–14 [Heb.]	73
2:8b–9 [Heb.]	70
2:9	72, 73, 82, 94
2:9 [Heb.]	70
2:10–17 [Heb.]	15, 72–75
2:10–16	13
2:10	72, 97, 119
2:10 [Heb.]	72, 90
2:11	11, 72–73, 73, 94
2:11b	72, 82
2:12	73, 78
2:12 [Heb.]	10, 72
2:13	73
2:13 [Heb.]	72, 94, 119
2:14 [Heb.]	72, 97
2:15 [Heb.]	11, 72–73, 94
2:16 [Heb.]	73, 78
2:17 [Heb.]	73
3:1–10	16, 18, 76–79
3:1	66, 76
3:2–10	77
3:2	76
3:3	76
3:4	76, 78
3:5	76
3:6	76
3:7–10	77
3:7	76–77
3:8	77, 93
3:9	77, 83, 137
3:10	77
4:1–14	16, 80–83
4:1–10	94
4:1–6	5
4:1	66, 80
4:2–14	81
4:2	80
4:3	80
4:4	80
4:5	80
4:6–10	81
4:6b–10a	81
4:6	11, 49, 80–81
4:7–10	58
4:7	81
4:8	81
4:9	74, 79, 81
4:10	5, 81
4:10b	79
4:11	81
4:12	81
4:13	81
4:14	81, 94
5:1–4	17, 84–85
5:1	84
5:2	66, 84, 87
5:3	84, 85

Scripture Index

5:4	84, 85, 103, 163	7:12	103
		8:1–8	19, 96–98
5:5–11	17, 86–88	8:1	96
5:5	66, 86, 87	8:2	67, 96, 124
5:6	86, 87	8:3	96, 97
5:7	86, 87	8:4	96
5:8	86, 87	8:5	96, 97
5:9	86, 88	8:6	96, 97
5:10	86	8:7	96
5:11	86–87, 88	8:8	96–97, 97
6:1–8	17	8:9–13	19, 99–101, 100
6:1	89		
6:2	89	8:9	99, 100
6:3	89	8:10–13	100
6:4–6	69	8:10	99
6:4	66, 89	8:11	99
6:5	73, 89	8:12	43, 99, 101
6:6	89	8:13	99–100, 100, 103
6:7	89, 90		
6:8	89, 90	8:14–17	19, 102–104, 103
6:9–15	14, 17, 83, 92–95, 93	8:14	102
6:9	92, 93	8:15	100, 102, 103
6:10	92, 93		
6:11	92, 94	8:16–17	103
6:12	79, 92	8:16	102, 103, 105, 106
6:12b–13	93		
6:13	92	8:17	102
6:14	92–93, 94	8:18–19	105–106
6:15	13, 65, 74, 82, 93	8:18	105
		8:19	103, 105
6:15a	94	8:20–23	107–109
6:15b	94	8:20–22	108
7–8	18	8:20	107, 108
7:1–7	18	8:21	107, 108
7:1	14, 64	8:22	74, 94, 107, 108
7:3–4	106		
7:5	67	8:23	107, 108
7:8–14	19, 103	9–14	14, 20, 21
7:9	103	9–11	22, 114
7:10	103	9–10	2

191

Zechariah (continued)

9:1–17	21
9:1–10	21
9:1–8	21, 22, 113–116, 114
9:1	113, 114
9:2	113
9:3	113
9:4	113
9:5	113–114, 114, 115
9:6	114, 115
9:7	114
9:8	114
9:9–17	22, 117–121
9:9–10	120
9:9	117, 120
9:10	90, 117, 124
9:11—11:3	21
9:11	117, 118
9:12	117–118, 118, 119
9:13–15	120
9:13	21, 118, 124
9:14	118
9:15	118
9:16	118, 119
9:17	118, 119
10:1–2	22
10:1	101
10:2	12, 123
10:3–12	23, 122–126
10:3	122, 123, 124
10:4	122, 123
10:5	122
10:6–7	119
10:6	122–123
10:6a	124
10:7	123, 124
10:8	123
10:9	123
10:10	123
10:10a	124
10:11	123
10:11c	124
10:12	123
10:12a	124
11:1–3	23
11:1	123
11:3	129
11:4–17	23, 25, 127–31, 129
11:4–16	21, 129
11:4–5	129
11:4	127
11:5	127, 129
11:6	127, 129
11:7	127
11:8	127
11:9	127–128
11:10	128
11:11	128
11:12–14	24
11:12	128
11:13	128, 131
11:14	128, 129
11:15	128
11:16	128, 129
11:17	128, 129
12–14	21, 22
12:1–6	24, 143
12:1	114
12:3–4	134
12:3	133
12:4	133, 141
12:6–9	142
12:6	133, 142
12:7–14	24, 132–135
12:7	132, 142
12:8	132, 133, 142

12:9	132, 133, 142	14:14–16	141
		14:14	140
12:10	22, 132, 133, 134, 135, 137	14:15	140
		14:16	141
		14:17	141
12:11	132–133, 133	14:18	141
		14:19	141
12:12	133	14:20	141
12:13–14	134	14:21	141, 144
12:13	133		
12:14	133	## Malachi	
13:1–6	25, 136–138		
13:1	133, 136, 137	1:2–5	7, 27, 147–149
13:2	130, 133, 136, 137	1:2–3	148
		1:2	147, 161
13:3	133, 136, 137	1:3	147
		1:4	147
13:4	133, 136–137, 137	1:5	147, 148, 153
13:5	137	1:6—2:9	27, 150–55
13:6	137	1:6–14	152
13:7–9	25, 130	1:6–7	161
13:9	162	1:6	148, 150, 158
14:1–21	139–144		
14:1–4a	141	1:7	148, 150
14:1	139, 141	1:8	26, 150
14:2	139	1:9	150
14:3	139	1:10	150–151, 152
14:4	139		
14:5b–9	141	1:11	151, 152, 153
14:5	139–140		
14:6	140, 142	1:12	151, 152
14:7	140	1:13	151, 152
14:8	140	1:14	151
14:9	140	2:1–9	152
14:10	140	2:1	151
14:11	140, 141, 171	2:2	151
		2:3–4	161
14:12	140	2:3	151
14:13	140, 141	2:4	151
		2:5	151

Malachi (continued)

2:6	151
2:7	151–152
2:8	152
2:9	152
2:10–16	27, 156–159
2:10–12	157
2:10	12, 156, 158
2:11	156
2:12	156, 157
2:13–16	157
2:13–14	148
2:13	156, 157
2:14	156–157
2:15	157, 158
2:16	157
2:17–3:12	27, 160–164
2:17	148, 157, 160, 161, 162
3:1–6	157
3:1	26, 160, 164
3:2	160, 164
3:3	160, 164
3:4	160–161
3:5	161
3:6	161
3:7–8	161
3:7	148, 161
3:8	148, 161
3:9	161
3:10	161, 166
3:11	161
3:12	161, 162
3:13–18	28, 165–167
3:13	148, 161, 165, 166
3:14	165
3:15	165, 169
3:16	165
3:17–18	169
3:17	165
3:18	165–166, 166, 169
3:19–21 [Heb.]	28, 168–169
3:19 [Heb.]	168, 169
3:20 [Heb.]	168
3:21	168
3:21 [Heb.]	169
3:22–24 [Heb.]	170–172
3:22 [Heb.]	170
3:23 [Heb.]	170
3:24 [Heb.]	170
4:1–3	28, 168–169
4:1	168, 169
4:2	168
4:3	168, 169
4:4–6	170–172
4:4	170

APOCRYPHA

Sirach

48:1–11	171
49:10	9

1 Maccabees

9:27	10
14:9	97
14:12	79
14:27	38

NEW TESTAMENT

Matthew

1:12	38
1:23	46, 108
3:4	79, 138
4:1–11	77

4:7	163
5:32	159
10:34–36	121
11:10	162
11:11–14	171
11:16–19	171
16:23	77
17:10–13	171
21:1–9	120
21:12–13	144
23	135
23:29–35	134
23:35	14, 22
25:32–33	125
26:15	131
27:3–10	131
28:20	46

Mark

1:2	162
1:6	138
1:12–13	77
3:8	149
8:27–30	95
8:33	77
9:11–13	171
9:11–12	171
10:2–12	159
10:11	159
11:1–10	120

Luke

1:5	95
1:16–17	171
2:14	121
2:25–38	67
3:27	38
3:31	134
4:1–13	77
7:27	162
14:28–30	83
19:29–38	120

John

2:13–22	144
4:1–42	38
4:7–26	75
4:21–24	44
10:12	130
12:12–15	120
19:34–37	134

Acts

5:33–39	58
8:4–8	75
8:9	163
8:26–38	75
10	75
10:22	74
10:35	153
13:6	163
18:7	74
18:6	75

Romans

9:13	148
15:1	50

1 Corinthians

7:10–11	159
16:13	50

2 Corinthians

12:10	50
13:9	50

Ephesians

6:10	50

Scripture Index

2 Timothy

2:1	50

Hebrews

12:26–27	52

1 Peter

2:9	167

Revelation

3:4–5	78
3:4	78
7:14	78
18:6	120
19:8	78
20:12	167
21:23	71
21:24	52
22:1–2	143
22:5	142

www.ingramcontent.com/pod-product-compliance
Lightning Source LLC
Chambersburg PA
CBHW021726220426
43662CB00008B/730